IMAGES
of America

VICKSBURG NATIONAL MILITARY PARK

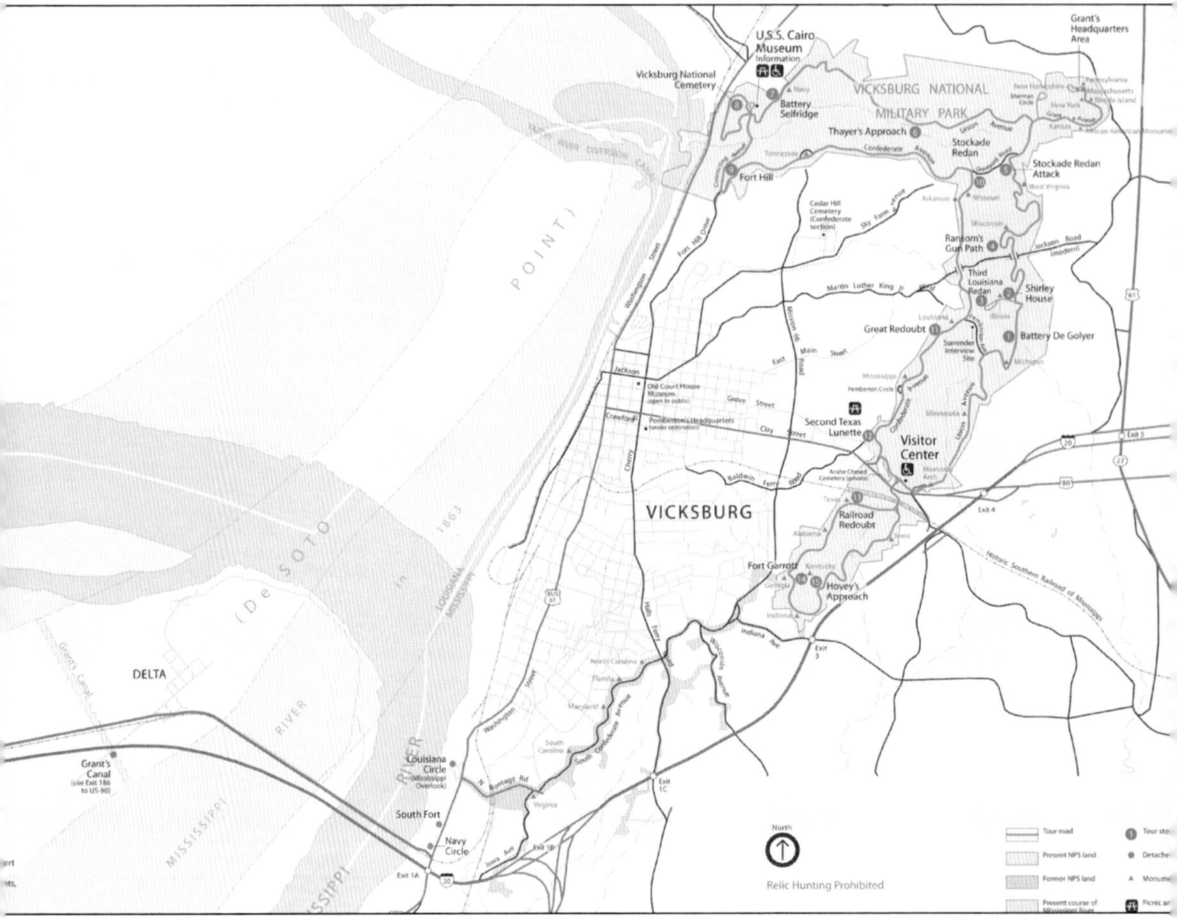

This present-day map shows the location of Vicksburg National Military Park within the community of Vicksburg. (Courtesy of Vicksburg National Military Park.)

On the Cover: The largest and most ornate monument to grace Vicksburg National Military Park is the Illinois Memorial, which was dedicated in a formal ceremony on October 26, 1906. Members of the Illinois National Guard parade along Jackson Road, proudly displaying their colors as they reach the site of the dedication. A vast crowd assembled to hear dignitaries from Illinois, Louisiana, and Mississippi give honor to the gallant soldiers from the Sucker State who participated in the most decisive campaign of the Civil War. (Courtesy of Vicksburg National Military Park.)

IMAGES
of America

VICKSBURG NATIONAL MILITARY PARK

Terrence J. Winschel

ARCADIA
PUBLISHING

ISBN 978-1-4671-1336-6

Published by Arcadia Publishing
Charleston, South Carolina

Printed in the United States of America

Library of Congress Control Number: 2014946152

For all general information, please contact Arcadia Publishing:
Telephone 843-853-2070
Fax 843-853-0044
E-mail sales@arcadiapublishing.com
For customer service and orders:
Toll-Free 1-888-313-2665

Visit us on the Internet at www.arcadiapublishing.com

To William T. Rigby, Albert P. Scheller, Edwin C. Bearss, and William O. Nichols, who have inspired and supported my stewardship of Vicksburg National Military Park

Contents

Acknowledgments

The author expresses his gratitude to R. Michael Madell, superintendent of Vicksburg National Military Park, and chief of operations Rick Martin. Heartfelt thanks are especially extended to staff members Virginia DuBowy and Elizabeth Joyner for the assistance they provided in accessing and scanning photographs in the park's extensive collection. This volume was made possible largely by their efforts. Unless otherwise noted, images appear courtesy of Vicksburg National Military Park. Thanks are also extended to Bubba Bolm, director of the Old Court House Museum (OCM) in Vicksburg, and the Mississippi Department of Archives and History (MDAH) for use of photographs from their collections. I am especially grateful to my wife, Therese, who has lived with my obsession and passion for history for more than 30 years. I love you.

Introduction

The Mississippi River in the mid-19th century has been accurately portrayed by biographer Lloyd Lewis as being "the spinal column of America . . . the symbol of geographic unity." He refers to the great river as "the trunk of the American tree, with limbs and branches reaching to the Alleghenies, the Canadian border, the Rocky Mountains." For more than 2,000 miles, the river flows silently on its course to the sea, providing a natural artery of commerce. Gliding along its muddy waters en route to world markets were steamers and flatboats of all descriptions, heavily laden with the rich agricultural produce of the land. Indeed, the silent water of the mighty river was then—as it remains to this day—the single most important economic feature of the continent, the very lifeblood of America. One contemporary wrote emphatically, "The valley of the Mississippi is America."

Upon the secession of the Southern states, and in particular Louisiana and Mississippi, the river was closed to unfettered navigation, which threatened to strangle Northern commercial interests. With the advent of the Civil War, Pres. Abraham Lincoln assembled his civil and military leaders to discuss strategy for opening the Mississippi River and ending what he termed a "rebellion" in the Southern states. Seated around a large table examining a map of the nation, Lincoln made a wide, sweeping gesture with his hand and then placed his finger on the map and said, "See what a lot of land these fellows hold, of which Vicksburg is the key. The war can never be brought to a close until that key is in our pocket."

As vital as the river was to the North, it was equally important to the South as a means of communication, transportation, and supply. To defend it, the Confederates fortified key points along the Mississippi, the most important of which was Vicksburg. The city's geographical location made it ideal for defense, as it was nestled along bluffs that tower almost 300 feet above a horseshoe-shaped bend of the river. Equally important, existing rail lines—which connected Vicksburg with Jackson and, via Jackson, points elsewhere in the Confederacy—enabled the shipment of heavy ordnance to the "Hill City," as it was known. These guns were trained on the river and posed the major obstacle to Union domination of the Mississippi. Vicksburg quickly became known as the "Gibraltar of the Confederacy," and it proved a tough nut to crack.

To seize Vicksburg and open the great river, the North assembled a powerful array of land and naval forces eager to confront the difficult task before them. With a vengeance, these forces moved from two directions in a massive converging attack to wrestle control of the river from Confederate troops. Driving south from Cairo, Illinois, Federal forces seized Forts Henry and Donelson, on the Tennessee and Cumberland Rivers, respectively, and opened the pathway of invasion to the Deep South. Continuing the drive, Union forces gained victory at Shiloh in April, Corinth in May, and, having forced the surrender of Island No. 10, seized Memphis in June.

Moving upriver from the Gulf of Mexico were ships of the West Gulf Blockading Squadron commanded by then flag officer David Glasgow Farragut. His ships bombarded and passed Forts Jackson and St. Philip on April 24 and compelled the surrender of New Orleans, the South's largest city. With initial success behind him, Farragut sent an advance flotilla upriver. Baton Rouge fell to the Federals on May 8, then Natchez, Mississippi, four days later, and the flotilla steamed on to Vicksburg. But, initial demands for the city's surrender were refused, as the post commander replied, "Mississippians don't know, and refuse to learn, how to surrender to an enemy." Despite being joined by the gunboats that came downriver from Memphis, the Union fleets were unable to reduce the city based solely on the might of their guns, and they withdrew in late July. The fortress city of Vicksburg would remain defiant for another year.

Late that year, Maj. Gen. Ulysses S. Grant was given the task of capturing Vicksburg. However, months of frustration and failure plagued his efforts, and by the spring of 1863 he was running out of time and options. Unable to reach Vicksburg by a northern approach, the Union commander boldly launched his army on a march south through Louisiana from his base camps at Milliken's Bend and Young's Point in search of a favorable crossing point somewhere below Vicksburg. As the soldiers slogged their way south over muddy roads, Rear Admiral David Dixon Porter, who commanded the Union fleet working in conjunction with Grant, prepared for a daring run past the batteries of Vicksburg. In a fiery exchange with Confederate shore batteries, Porter's gunboats and army transports managed to pass below Vicksburg on April 16 and rendezvoused with Grant. On April 30–May 1, the Union army was hurled across the river and onto Mississippi soil at Bruinsburg and began the inland campaign to capture Vicksburg.

Over the next 17 days, Grant's forces pushed deep into Mississippi, gained victory over Confederate forces in five separate battles, and drove the Southern army under Lt. Gen. John C. Pemberton back into the city's formidable defenses. Union assaults on May 19 and 22 were easily and bloodily repulsed. Failing to take the city by storm, Grant decided to "outcamp the enemy" and laid siege to the city. Cut off from all supply and communication with the outside world, the citizens and soldiers of Vicksburg had to subsist on what had been stockpiled in the city prior to the siege. With each passing day, those supplies dwindled. Sickness spread like wildfire, and death was ever present as citizens and soldiers alike fell victim to Union sharpshooters and artillery fire that rained down upon the city for 47 days.

Finally, on July 4, white flags appeared along the lines, and the valiant defenders of Vicksburg marched forth from their works, stacked their arms, and furled their flags in surrender. Victorious Union forces took possession of the city that had eluded them for so long. A jubilant President Lincoln declared, "The Father of Waters again flows unvexed to the sea." The Union victory at Vicksburg was the most decisive of the war, as it gave the North control of the river, cut the Confederacy in two, and effectively sealed the doom of Richmond, the Confederate capital.

To commemorate the campaign, siege, and defense of Vicksburg, Congress established Vicksburg National Military Park, which encompasses approximately 1,800 acres and includes the hallowed ground of Vicksburg National Cemetery. Each year, the park attracts hundreds of thousands of visitors to Vicksburg, who come from all 50 states and scores of foreign lands; however, few who visit realize that the park has a rich and fascinating history all its own. The pages that follow document in words and with photographs the early, formative years of the park during which time the land was purchased, roads and bridges were constructed to allow for visitor access, and hundreds of monuments, markers, tablets, and plaques were erected to honor the men in blue and gray who in the crucible of war experienced the most terrifying ordeal of their lives in the struggle for national identity.

One

Creating an American Shrine

In the closing years of the 19th century, as the generation that fought the Civil War departed to answer the final roll call in response to Gabriel's trumpet, veterans who once wore the blue and gray banded together and moved to preserve the fields of battle on which they had fought. As governors' mansions and statehouses across the nation, as well as Congress and the White House itself, were still dominated by Civil War veterans, such noble sentiment was quickly acted upon. In 1890, Congress set aside the battlefields around Chattanooga, Tennessee, as the nation's first national military park. Establishment of Antietam National Battlefield in Maryland, site of the single bloodiest day of combat in American military history, quickly followed. In 1894, the battlefield at Shiloh was also set aside by Congress, and in 1895 Gettysburg was declared a national military park.

The same spirit of nationalism that led to the establishment of these parks inspired thousands of Union and Confederate veterans to gather in Vicksburg in May 1890 for the Blue and Gray Reunion. Jointly sponsored by Camp 32 of the United Confederate Veterans and Grand Army of the Republic Post 7, both of Vicksburg, the weeklong event drew veterans and politicians from across the country. Those in attendance were saddened to see the battlefield at Vicksburg all but forgotten. Although many of the forts and long lines of trenches that had played such a significant role in the 47-day siege of the city in 1863 were still visible, no effort to preserve them was evident. The former soldiers left Vicksburg convinced that the fields on which they had fought and thousands of their comrades had died "deserved more and must be properly marked and preserved by our government."

In October 1895, veterans from the North and South once again met in Vicksburg. Led by John F. Merry of Iowa and Stephen D. Lee of Mississippi, they formed the Vicksburg National Military Park Association and for the next several years labored to seek establishment by Congress of a national military park at Vicksburg.

Following the Civil War and the era of Reconstruction, a man named Tom Lewis attempted to initiate local efforts to preserve the forts and long lines of earthworks that still ringed the city. Although Lewis circulated petitions throughout Vicksburg and escorted people around the battlefield, his efforts failed to spur the elected officials into action. If the battlefield at Vicksburg was to be preserved for the benefit of future generations, it was obvious that Congressional action was necessary and that only the veterans themselves could succeed in this effort. Although Northern veterans would be quick to support such an effort, to be successful it would also require the support of former Confederate soldiers—not just those in Mississippi, but from across the South. In this photograph, Lewis stands at the entrance to the cave behind his house on Grove Street that sheltered him throughout the 47-day siege of Vicksburg. (OCM.)

Credited as the "father of the Vicksburg park idea," John F. Merry was a native of Peninsula, Ohio, born on March 24, 1844. His family migrated to Iowa in 1856 and settled in Delaware County. In August 1862, he enlisted in the 21st Iowa Infantry, but he was discharged for disability in March 1863. He reenlisted in April 1864 in the 46th Iowa Infantry, but saw no action. Following the war, Merry became captain of the Governor's Greys, a ceremonial militia unit. In 1894, while returning from a parade in New Orleans, the Greys stopped in Vicksburg. Although it was a goodwill visit, Merry's principal objective was to sound out Southern veterans and the people of the Hill City as to their views on the establishment of a national military park at Vicksburg. He secured the support of former Confederate lieutenant general Stephen D. Lee, and together they spurred Union and Confederate veterans to form the Vicksburg National Military Park Association.

Born in Charleston, South Carolina, on September 22, 1833, Stephen D. Lee was a West Point graduate, class of 1854. At the outbreak of the Civil War, he entered Confederate service as a captain and aide-de-camp to Gen. P.G.T. Beauregard and rose to become the youngest lieutenant general in Confederate service. After the war, he resided in Mississippi, where he was a planter, state senator, and first president of what is today Mississippi State University. Lee was also a spokesman for Southern veterans and embraced the New South philosophy. As Lee demonstrated a willingness to work with former enemies in the interest of a unified nation, Merry considered his participation vital to gain Southern support for the park idea. Lee was enthusiastic about the idea. Although defeat at Vicksburg had sealed the doom of the Confederacy, the general believed that the Southern soldiers who had fought so valiantly at Vicksburg deserved to be honored rather than shadowed by shame. He promised both his support and energies on behalf of the enterprise and agreed to the formation of the Vicksburg National Military Park Association.

On November 19, 1895, the charter of incorporation for the Vicksburg National Military Park Association was signed by Gov. John M. Stone and issued by Secretary of State George M. Govan of Mississippi. Stone had been colonel of the 2nd Mississippi Infantry during the war and in the aftermath of conflict served as governor of Mississippi from 1876 to 1882 and again from 1890 to 1896. (MDAH.)

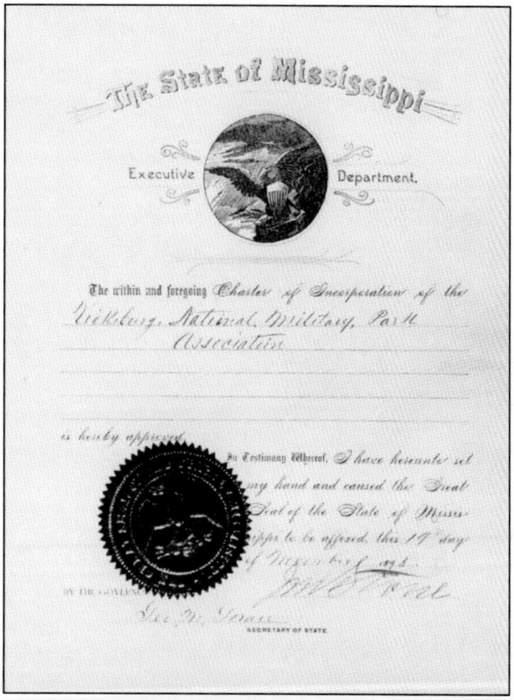

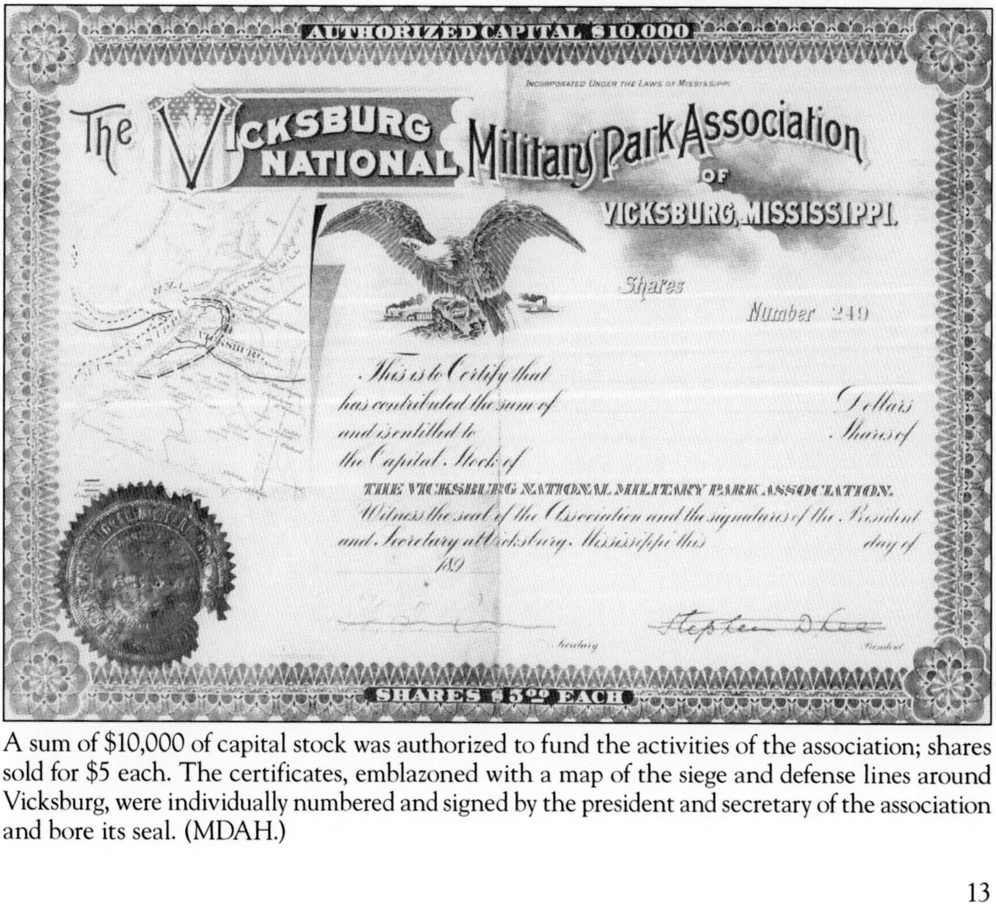

A sum of $10,000 of capital stock was authorized to fund the activities of the association; shares sold for $5 each. The certificates, emblazoned with a map of the siege and defense lines around Vicksburg, were individually numbered and signed by the president and secretary of the association and bore its seal. (MDAH.)

On October 22, 1895, a preliminary meeting of the association, called by Captain Merry, was held in the club room of the New Pacific House on Washington Street in Vicksburg. Lee was elected chairman, addresses were made by Lee, Merry, and others, and plans were outlined for a permanent organization. The purpose of the association was to petition Congress to establish a national military park at Vicksburg. Lee was elected president of the new organization. The other officers were Charles Davidson, formerly of the 25th Iowa Infantry, vice-president; William T. Rigby, former captain in the 24th Iowa Infantry, secretary; and Charles Conway Flowerree of Mississippi, former colonel of the 7th Virginia Infantry, treasurer. When the association formed there in 1895, the New Pacific House was one of Vicksburg's most popular hotels and advertised that its "cuisine [was] unsurpassed." Commonly called the "Piazza Hotel" as its proprietor was Vincent Piazza, the New Pacific House opened in 1893. Renamed the National Park Hotel, it is shown here gaily bedecked to greet Pres. Theodore Roosevelt in 1907. The hotel was torn down in 1972. (OCM.)

William T. Rigby (seated) and Charles Flowerree served a secretary and treasurer, respectively, of the Vicksburg National Military Park Association. Rigby was born in Red Oak Grove, Iowa, on November 3, 1841. Appointed second lieutenant in Company B, 24th Iowa Infantry in September 1862, he was promoted to captain of the company on October 2, 1863, and served in that capacity until the end of the war. After being mustered out of service, he entered Cornell College in Mount Vernon, Iowa, and graduated in 1872. At the urging of his brother-in-law John Merry, Rigby joined the park movement and from the moment of its inception proved the most dedicated, energetic, and committed member of the association. Flowerree was a native of Fauquier County, Virginia, born on October 26, 1842. He was a cadet at Virginia Military Institute when war erupted and entered Confederate service as a member of the 7th Virginia Infantry, of which regiment he rose to become colonel. After the war, he moved to Mississippi and became president of the Vicksburg Ice Company and served as Vicksburg's postmaster from 1893 until 1897.

Members of the Vicksburg National Military Park Association Board of Directors and its executive committee posed for this photograph in front of the historic Warren County Courthouse in October 1895. The board of directors included such prominent men as William D. Hoard, former governor of Wisconsin; John M. Stone, governor of Mississippi; Frederick Dent Grant, son of Gen. Ulysses S. Grant; Thomas N. Waul, former Confederate general who commanded Waul's Texas Legion at Vicksburg; Lucius Fairchild, governor of Wisconsin; Russell Alger, secretary of war; John B. Gordon, commander of the United Confederate Veterans; and Edmund Pettus, former Confederate general and US senator from Alabama. Standing at center is former Confederate lieutenant general Stephen D. Lee, who served as president of the association. Charles Davidson, sitting at far left, was vice president. Sitting next to Davidson is William T. Rigby, the association's secretary, and sitting second from right is its treasurer, Charles Conway Flowerree.

Although the association formed at the New Pacific House on Washington Street, all subsequent meetings of the members were held in the parlors of the Carroll Hotel that stood on the southwest corner of Clay and Walnut Streets. Named in honor of E.C. Carroll, a prominent local businessman of the Anchor Line of steamboats, it too opened in 1893 and proudly offered 100 "luxuriously furnished rooms equipped with all the modern conveniences." The hotel housed six shops on the ground floor, along with a billiard room, baggage rooms and storerooms, a reading room, and a grand rotunda. The parlor rooms were also exquisitely furnished and well suited for meetings of the association. Although luxurious, the hotel boasted that its "prices will be found eminently reasonable." The building was taken down in 1963, and a parking garage was built on its site. (OCM.)

Thomas C. Catchings (at left), a Confederate veteran who served as US representative from Mississippi's Third Congressional District, introduced the park bill in 1896. His bill, however, died when the 54th Congress adjourned in March 1897. Catchings again determined to act in the 55th Congress. On December 9, 1897, he introduced a bill "to establish a national military park to commemorate the campaign, siege, and defense of Vicksburg." It was not until February 6, 1899, that the bill was read by the clerk, voted on, and passed unanimously. Two days later, Sen. Edmund Pettus (below) of Alabama, who had served under Lee's command at Vicksburg, sent to the floor a companion bill. On February 10, the measure was read and passed. It was signed by Pres. William McKinley on February 21.

Two

A Legacy of Service

"Vicksburg National Military Park Bill Passed the Senate Today," blazed the headlines of the *Vicksburg Evening Post* on February 10, 1899, and the publication confidently asserted that the bill would "now be signed by the president." Although temperatures in the city plummeted below zero that day, the citizens of Vicksburg hailed passage of the bill. "The Park will be a great thing for Vicksburg," editorialized the paper, "it will be a source of pleasure to our own people, and will annually attract thousands of visitors from various parts of the Nation." Eleven days later, Pres. William McKinley affixed his signature to the bill by which the battlefield at Vicksburg became a national military park. Indeed, there was cause for celebration and pride in the city and across the nation, especially among those whose service and sacrifice would now be memorialized.

Secretary of War Russell Alger appointed a three-man commission to oversee the establishment of the park and conduct its operations. The three men had been active members of the Vicksburg National Military Park Association and traveled to Washington to receive their appointments. After receiving their commissions from Secretary Alger, the three men met next in Vicksburg, where they arrived on March 14 to establish the park office and start their new duties. A topographical survey was ordered of the lands to be acquired, tracts were purchased, and exhaustive correspondence was conducted with veterans of the siege to amass information necessary to accurately mark the battlefield with historical tablets for the benefit of visitors. More than 125 Civil War–era cannon were requisitioned from the Quartermaster Department and mounted in the field to mark the locations of Union and Confederate batteries during the siege and defense of the city. The commissioners worked tirelessly to construct roads and bridges and secure the placement of monuments by the various states represented by troops during the siege and defense of Vicksburg. Throughout these efforts, the commissioners desired that both sides be treated fairly in the presentation during the siege. Their efforts resulted in Vicksburg's becoming one of the finest military parks in the world.

The legislation by which the park was established called for the appointment of three commissioners to oversee it. All three had to be veterans of the Vicksburg campaign, with one Confederate representative and two Union representatives. Lee was clearly the logical choice for the Confederate representative, and his appointment was quickly made by the secretary of war. As more than 36,000 Illinois soldiers served in the Vicksburg campaign, making up a full half of Grant's army that captured the "Gibraltar of the Confederacy," it was readily accepted that someone from Illinois must serve on the commission. Thus, James Everest, a former captain of Company I, 13th Illinois Infantry, was appointed as one of the Union representatives. In recognition of his work to secure establishment of the park, the association's dedicated secretary, William Rigby of Iowa, gained the coveted final appointment to the commission. From left to right in this photograph taken on March 15, 1899, when the commission held its first meeting in Vicksburg, are commissioners James G. Everest, William T. Rigby, and chairman Stephen D. Lee.

The commissioners were authorized to appoint a historian and secretary. Photographed in Vicksburg with the park commissioners on March 15, 1899, are John S. Kountz (standing at left) and Charles L. Longley (sitting at right), who served as historian and secretary, respectively, of the park commission. Kountz was born in Maumee, Ohio, in 1846, and had served as a musician in Company G, 37th Ohio Infantry during the war. At Missionary Ridge on November 25, 1863, the young drummer boy picked up a rifle musket and voluntarily went into action. In the fighting, Kountz was severely wounded, which resulted in the amputation of his right leg. For his bravery that day, he was awarded the Medal of Honor. In the aftermath of war, Kountz served as commander in chief of the Grand Army of the Republic. Longley was a native of Massachusetts but resided in Tipton, Iowa, when war erupted in 1861. He enlisted in the 24th Iowa Infantry and served with William T. Rigby. This association led to his appointment as secretary of the park commission.

For the first several weeks, the commissioners worked out of the Carroll Hotel until a suitable office space could be secured. Captain Rigby arranged to rent the home of Pauline Rice, which was located on the northeast corner of Clay and Cherry Streets. (The Rice family ran a furniture store on Washington Street but had recently opened a new store in Birmingham and moved to Alabama.) In this photograph, taken in October 1901, commissioners Lee and Rigby (standing second and third from left) and secretary Longley (standing top row center) are pictured in front of the park office with Union and Confederate veterans from Missouri. Former Confederate general Francis M. Cockrell, who at this time was a powerful US senator from Missouri, is the bearded man sitting on the rocker in front. The park office remained at 100 North Cherry Street until 1909, when it was moved to Drummond Street.

Among the first duties performed by the commissioners was the completion of a survey of the land to be included in the park. The enabling legislation specified that the park would consist of a main body from which "wings" radiated to the Mississippi River above and below Vicksburg. The main body ran north along the former Union siege and Confederate defense lines from Fort Garrott to Thayer's Approach and included all the ground in between the positions of the opposing armies. (This was the area in which the Union assaults of May 19 and 22, 1863, had occurred.) From the main body, narrow strips of land would be secured for the construction of roads and placement of monuments and tablets: "The whole containing about one thousand two hundred acres, and costing not to exceed forty thousand dollars." Pictured here are the men who made up the first survey party: W.F. King, J.L. Cash, P.M. Polk, and G.C. Hayden.

On May 21–22, 1908, Union veterans of the 22nd Iowa Infantry, some of whom were the very men that pierced the Confederate defenses at Railroad Redoubt on May 22, 1863, held a reunion at Vicksburg and invited former Confederate general Stephen D. Lee to attend. Although his health was broken, Lee traveled to Vicksburg, where he arrived on Thursday, May 21, and stayed at the home of his friend and fellow commissioner Captain Rigby. The general spent Friday in the company of Union veterans and that afternoon delivered a "fervid and patriotic" address in which he praised the bravery of his former enemies and extolled the spirit of nationalism that characterized America in the early 20th century. Having spoken with energy and passion, he was emotionally and physically drained by day's end. Still, Lee agreed to pose for a picture, but urged the photographer to hurry as he "felt badly" and wanted to return to the city. Lee, standing second from left, died within days of posing for this photograph.

Following a light dinner on Friday evening, May 22, 1908, Lee was crippled by a severe attack of indigestion and placed in bed. Dr. J.A.K. Birchett was called to the Rigby home on Cherry Street to administer medication. The patient responded to treatment and appeared to improve over the next few days; however, on Tuesday, May 26, his condition grew worse, and that night he slipped into a coma from which he never awoke. At 6:00 a.m. on Thursday, May 28, the gallant warrior breathed his last. The Vicksburg paper lamented his loss in headlines, which read, "General S.D. Lee's Great Heart Beats No More. Commander-in-Chief U.C.V. Is Dead." The body of General Lee, dressed in civilian clothes and placed in a black coffin that was covered with the Stars and Bars of the Confederacy, was made available for public display at the park office. Hundreds of mourners, many of whom were veterans of the Blue and Gray, paraded by his coffin as if on review and paid their final respects.

The furious pace required of the commissioners, and of Lee and Rigby in particular, had quickly exhausted the general. On December 20, 1899, he had written to Secretary of War Elihu Root asking to be temporarily relieved from his duties as chairman of the park commission and recommending that Captain Rigby be named acting chairman. As his health continued to deteriorate, Lee was forced to conduct less and less park business. He reluctantly accepted the limitations that age and health were forcing upon him and on November 21, 1901, tendered his resignation as chairman of the commission to Captain Rigby. Lee, however, remained on the commission as the Confederate representative and continued to work on behalf of the park until his death in 1908. His position on the commission was filled by Lewis Guion (pictured here), former captain of Company D, 26th Louisiana Infantry. Guion, however, was the next member of the commission to pass away, dying on January 12, 1920.

Three

Early Park Landscape

In the summer of 1862, the decision was made to construct a line of defense to guard the city's landward approaches. Design and construction of these works was assigned to Maj. Samuel Lockett. Working under Lockett's supervision, the Confederate garrison and thousands of slaves pressed into service were put to work clearing vast tracts of forest to construct fortifications, clear fields of fire, and form a dense obstruction of felled trees in front of their works. In similar fashion, when the Union army assumed its position around Vicksburg, Northern soldiers cut extensive tracts of forest to open avenues of approach and construct a battery position. Thus, the area between the battle lines was void of vegetation, and the opposing forces had a clear, unobstructed view of one another along their entire length. During the siege, the movement of troops, approach operations, and constant artillery firing left the battlefield a desolate moonscape.

In the years following the siege, citizens returned to the area around Vicksburg and resumed farming practices. As the landscape had been cleared by the armies, local farmers were able to cultivate the land, and extensive grazing of cattle, sheep, hogs, and horses kept the hillsides largely tree free for the remainder of the 19th century. Thus, when the park commissioners began their work, they found the battlefield much in keeping with its wartime appearance. The early photographs of the park provide powerful evidence of the open landscape that enabled returning veterans to easily identify where their units had been positioned during the siege and defense of Vicksburg and assist the commissioners in placing the monuments, markers, tablets, and plaques that make Vicksburg one of the more accurately marked battlefields in the world.

Dramatic changes to the landscape, especially in terms of vegetation, occurred in the 1930s through the work of the Civilian Conservation Corps. These changes, which will be covered in chapter nine, have transformed much of the battlefield into a dense forest. Thus, the landscape today bears little resemblance to its appearance when the park was managed by the US War Department.

On July 3, 1863, the 46th day of siege, Generals John C. Pemberton and Ulysses S. Grant met between the lines near Jackson Road to discuss surrender terms. Although the two commanders failed to reach agreement and returned to their respective headquarters, they did come to terms later that night through an exchange of notes. At 10:00 a.m. on July 4, white flags appeared along the lines. The siege of Vicksburg was over, and the "Father of Waters," as President Lincoln expressed it, "again flows unvexed to the sea." This stone shaft erected by Union occupation forces in July 1864, on the anniversary of the city's surrender, was the first monument placed on the battlefield; it marked the site of the surrender interview between two generals on July 3, 1863.

In its then isolated location, the Surrender Interview Monument suffered frequent damage by souvenir hunters who chipped out pieces of stone with their penknives. In 1867, the marble shaft was moved to the train station in town, where it was hoped the flux of visitors would prevent further damage. Sadly, the monument was only exposed to additional vandalism. In 1868, the shaft was moved once more to Vicksburg National Cemetery, where it was hoped that the solemnity of the burial ground would help protect the monument. (The monument was returned to its original location in the 1940s, taken down again in 1988, and in the 1990s was placed on display in the park's Visitor Center.) This close-up of the Surrender Interview Monument atop the Indian Mound in Vicksburg National Cemetery shows the damage from souvenir hunters. In the background is Fort Hill, which was the northern anchor of the Confederate defense line around Vicksburg.

In 1867, when the stone shaft was moved to the train station in town, it was replaced at the Surrender Interview Site with a 42-pounder cannon placed upright in the ground. An appropriate inscription was etched into the barrel, but it gave the incorrect date of the meeting between Pemberton and Grant: July 4, 1863, rather than July 3. The cannon remained in place until the 1940s and was a popular attraction for visitors, such as those shown below in the late 19th or early 20th century. The cannon was declared surplus and transferred to another national park, where the inscription was filled in and painted over. More than four decades later, the cannon returned to Vicksburg, and the inscription was restored. The same cannon again replaced the marble shaft when it was taken down in 1988, and it once more stands at the Surrender Interview Site.

Hon. J. C. Pemberton, III. Col. U.S. Grant, III.

On May 22, 1937, the anniversary of Grant's second assault against the Vicksburg defenses, John C. Pemberton III and Ulysses S. Grant III met at the Surrender Interview Site and posed for this photograph shaking hands. The meeting between their grandfathers presented a stark contrast. General Grant recalled of Pemberton that nothing could put him at ease and he appeared "much excited." In response to the Union commander's demand for unconditional surrender, Pemberton snapped, "Then, sir, it is unnecessary that you and I should hold any further conversation; we will go to fighting again at once." Then, shaking his finger in Grant's face exclaimed, "I can assure you, sir, you will bury many more of your men before you will enter Vicksburg." The two generals parted without agreeing to terms.

The Confederate defense line consisted of nine major forts connected by a continuous line of trenches and rifle pits. The line stretched for more than eight miles and formed a huge crescent around Vicksburg. The flanks rested on the river above and below the city and guarded all land approaches, including the railroad access, into Vicksburg. Remnants of the once-formidable earthworks that defended the city were still extant when the park was established. Shown above is South Fort, the southern anchor of the Confederate defense line that guarded the Warrenton Road (at right) access to Vicksburg. Below is Square Fort, which is also known as Fort Garrott, named in honor of Brig. Gen. Isham Garrott, who was killed here by a Union sharpshooter on June 17, 1863.

Pictured here is the interior of the earthen fort called Stockade Redan. The remnants of the once-powerful Confederate bastion northeast of Vicksburg seemed to still stand guard along Graveyard Road (at left) in the late 1890s, when this photograph was taken. Here, on May 19 and 22, 1863, soldiers from Mississippi and Missouri repulsed determined Union assaults.

Stockade Redan is shown from the Union perspective in this photograph taken around 1906. The various stone monuments, such as the one to the 27th Ohio Infantry in the foreground, mark the farthest point reached by Union regiments in the attacks on May 19 and 22, 1863. The assaults were hurled back with heavy losses, compelling Grant to lay siege to the city.

This view of Jackson Road looking west was taken from the knoll on which the Illinois Monument now stands. Note how narrow the ridge is along which the road runs. The Union assault on May 22, 1863, was funneled through the narrow road cut, and men in blue were cut down by the hundreds. The knoll at left center is where Battery Hickenlooper was located.

This view looking east along Jackson Road toward the Shirley House was taken from the Third Louisiana Redan, one of two Confederate forts that guarded this entryway into Vicksburg. The Illinois Monument now stands on the knoll left of the Shirley House. The buildings in the foreground at right are all postwar structures.

Taken from the Third Louisiana Redan (present-day Tour Stop 3) looking north across the valley of Glass Bayou toward Graveyard Road, this stunning view highlights the topography that made Vicksburg a natural fortress. The city's natural defensibility was strengthened by Major Lockett's extensive network of earthen forts and rifle pits. It also illustrates that the park was virtually tree free in its early formative years and reflects the battlefield's wartime appearance.

This c. 1900 image of present-day Tour Stop 1 (Battery De Golyer) looks north toward the Shirley House, which is visible on the high ground in the center. The lunettes (crescent-shaped earthworks) that protected the guns and cannoneers during the long siege in 1863 are still visible to the right of the tree in the foreground. Battery De Golyer, with 22 guns, was the largest concentration of cannon along the Union siege lines. In 2011, the dense forest that covered this area of the park was removed to restore the field to its wartime appearance, and the site today very much resembles this photograph.

Remnants of the lunettes that shelter the guns and artillerymen of the 4th Ohio Battery were still visible along Union Avenue when this photograph was taken around 1900. The view is looking south across the headwaters of Mint Spring Bayou toward the ridge along which the Confederate defenses were located. At any point along the siege and defense lines, the opposing forces had a clear, unobstructed view of one another.

The US Navy Monument, dedicated in 1917, now stands on the high ground pictured here along Union Avenue. During the siege, large guns taken from the ironclad gunboat *Cincinnati* were mounted here in what was known as Battery Selfridge and were served by naval personnel.

In the center of the high ground in the distance is Railroad Redoubt. This Confederate bastion guarded the Southern Railroad of Mississippi, the tracks of which are seen at right, and was one of the nine major forts defending Vicksburg. This view is reflective of how the site looked on May 22, 1863, when Union troops surged through the ravine in the foreground and gained a temporary lodgment in the fort.

Located along Baldwin's Ferry Road at what was referred to as "Burnt Chimneys" was a Union battery served by cannoneers from Ohio and Indiana. The Indiana Monument, dedicated in 1926, stood on the knoll at right, and the area was named "Indiana Circle." The monument was moved, and "Indiana Circle" was removed to make way for the present-day Visitor Center and parking area.

Four

Safe and Beautiful Access

The enabling act charged the commissioners "to open and construct and to repair such roads as may be necessary" to provide for safe visitor access. As the military operations that focused on Vicksburg culminated in siege operations, there were two distinct battle lines: the Confederate defense line and the Union investment line. This made the layout of roads relatively simple, but terrain made construction difficult.

A study of the siege satisfied the commissioners that "Confederate Avenue should as closely as possible, follow the line of earthworks . . . and should, at all points, be in the rear thereof." These lines had been located by Confederate engineer Samuel Lockett on a continuous ridge, broken only by Glass and Stouts Bayous and the spot where the tracks of the Southern Railroad of Mississippi cut through it east of town. In the years since the war, Halls Ferry Road had been worn so deep by traffic and erosion as to require a bridge to cross it. Four bridges were therefore necessary on Confederate Avenue.

As the Union siege lines were in flux during the siege, the commissioners held that a line of investment should be established along the Union works within the portion of the park where the assaults of May 19 and 22 had occurred. (The assaults were made over a three-mile front that ran from Fort Garrott on the south to Thayer's Approach on the north.) "Reasonable convenience in studying the composition and deployment" of Union units involved a "continuous avenue along this part of the investment line." Unlike the Confederate rifle pits, the Union works did not follow a continuous ridge but crossed a succession of steep ridges and deep hollows. This was especially true on the Union left flank that stretched to the river below town. To avoid crossing four deep hollows, the commissioners determined "to constitute this wing by four separate spurs, with avenues along each"; these were known as Indiana, Wisconsin, Illinois, and Iowa Avenues.

Over the years, the network of roads and bridges network has provided a safe and beautiful means by which millions of visitors have enjoyed the solemnity and splendor of the park.

This bridge constructed in 1907 by the William T. Young Bridge Company of Nashville, Tennessee, spanned the tracks of the historic Southern Railroad of Mississippi and gave access to Maloney Circle. The impressive equestrian statue to Union major general John A. McClernand, along with several large cannon, was originally intended to be placed at Maloney Circle, which explains the reason for the bridge; however, the monument was placed elsewhere, and the guns were never mounted. Thus, few visitors to the park are familiar with this bridge, which is no longer open for vehicle traffic but stills stands opposite Old Highway 27 from the Vicksburg Convention and Visitors Bureau office.

Nine Melan arch bridges—identical in appearance but of varying lengths, all along Union Avenue—were constructed around 1903 by the William T. Young Bridge Company. In this photograph, the apron (or approach) is completed, and two workmen are taking a break after making the rectangular excavations for placement of the cheek (or sidewalls).

Workmen have completed the wooden forms for the center supports and the "drum" that will form the arch of this Melan bridge. Once the concrete was poured, the wooden forms were removed. Visitors who closely examine the underside of the arches can still see the imprint of the framing boards.

Framing of the cheek walls, or sidewalls, is completed, and the project is ready for concrete to be poured. Workmen who constructed the Melan arch bridges lived on site, and all nine bridges were completed within a year. Attesting to the durability of this design, eight of the nine bridges are still servicing park visitors.

The "drum," which forms the arch between the cheek walls, is reinforced with railroad iron. In this photograph, construction supervisors inspect the work thus far performed. Also visible at left in the cheek wall are the molds for decorative designs that add to the beauty of the park's Melan arch bridges.

Once the concrete, which was poured one wheelbarrow full at a time, had cured, the wooden forms for the cheek walls and "drum" were removed. The bridge form was then filled with dirt, as shown in this photograph of the Melan arch at present-day Tour Stop 6 (Thayer's Approach).

The final phase of construction on the Melan arch bridges was installation of the freestanding balustrade and decorative iron railings. Shown here soon after completion is historic Bridge No. 2 along North Union Avenue, looking south over the valley of Mint Spring Bayou toward the ridge along which the Confederate defense line stood.

Carriage tracks are visible in the dirt deck of Historic Bridge No. 3 in the foreground, with Bridge No. 2 in the distance. Towering above Union Avenue on the right is Belle Smith Ridge, from which location Union artillery fired over the valley of Mint Spring Bayou, on the left, and hammered the Confederate defenses.

Residents who frequently walk or jog on the park's South Loop will readily recognize these two Melan arch bridges. This is an area of the park once referred to as the "Reunion Grounds," the site of the National Memorial Celebration and Peace Jubilee in 1917, which is addressed in chapter eight.

Two bridges of identical design were constructed to span the tracks of the historic Southern Railroad of Mississippi: one on Confederate Avenue and the other on Union Avenue. Here, workmen prepare and place deck planks on the Confederate Avenue bridge. These bridges were removed as part of the Mission 66 project at the same time an underpass was constructed to carry park traffic below Clay Street.

One of only four bridges necessary along Confederate Avenue, this span over Stout's Bayou is the longest bridge constructed in the park. With the advent of the automobile, the bridge was realigned in the 1930s to eliminate the sharp curves of its eastern approach. The modern span is located at the south end of Confederate Avenue just west of the Vicksburg Little Theater.

Constructed in 1903 by the Penn Bridge Company, this arch truss bridge on Confederate Avenue spanned Glass Bayou and was used by park visitors until 1972, when an adjacent bridge was built and opened. Although the only extant example of a steel arch structure in Mississippi, the bridge was removed in the 1990s as it was in danger of imminent collapse.

This early park guardrail was constructed by the enrollees of the Civilian Conservation Corps (CCC) in the 1930s along Union Avenue just south of Graveyard Road. At left is a barracks building of one of the four CCC camps established at Vicksburg. This particular camp was MP-4.

Looking north over Glass Bayou from behind the Shirley House, this view of Bridge No. 5 clearly illustrates what the park looked like in its early, formative years. This bridge was removed as part of the Mission 66 program to enable construction of modern-day Jackson Road, which follows the course of Glass Bayou and runs between the city and Sherman Avenue Elementary School.

Here is a similar view of the valley of Glass Bayou and Bridge No. 5 looking south toward the Shirley House. This image, taken between 1902, when restoration of the Shirley House was completed, and 1905, when work on the Illinois monument (located to the right of the Shirley House) began, reveals the true nature of the park's landscape and the amount of work necessary to construct the roads and bridges.

Union Avenue, where it crosses the North Fork of Glass Bayou on Bridge No. 4, is seen winding its way north toward Graveyard Road and Stockade Redan, which crown the high ground at right. Also visible at right along the skyline are cannon that mark the positions of powerful Federal batteries that sent solid shot and shell crashing among the Confederate defenders.

A gentleman in a horse and buggy traveling south along Union Avenue crosses the North Fork of Glass Bayou on Bridge No. 4. Once situated between the Wisconsin Monument and Graveyard Road (present-day Tour Stops 4 and 5, respectively), the bridge was replaced with a box culvert in the 1970s.

Thanks to the road-and-bridge network constructed by the park commissioners in the early 1900s, the park has since its inception attracted millions of visitors (such as those shown here around 1905) from across the nation and around the world, providing them with safe and pleasant access whether on foot, by horse and buggy, or in modern automobiles and buses.

Visitors to the park in its early years had stunning views of the city of Vicksburg, especially from along Confederate Avenue. This view, taken from the intersection of Wisconsin Avenue and Confederate Avenue (present site of Toot's Grocery), reveals the near-barren nature of the hillsides around Vicksburg that was a direct result of the military operations of the Civil War.

Visitors driving west along Pemberton Avenue approaching the Surrender Interview Site are seen in this photograph taken by Vicksburg photographer J. Mack Moore around 1910. The obelisk that towers above the trees at right is the Minnesota Monument that was dedicated in 1907. Soldiers of the 4th Minnesota were the first to enter Vicksburg on July 4, 1863.

The statue of Union captain Andrew Hickenlooper, chief engineer of the XVII Corps, is admired by a visitor heading west on Jackson Road. The Illinois Monument is in the background, as are the cannon that mark the location of Battery Hickenlooper. Prior to the construction of US Highway 80, Jackson Road was the main thoroughfare between Vicksburg and Jackson.

Five

Shirley House and Other Park Structures

Built in the 1830s by Nicholas Gray, Wexford Lodge is the only surviving wartime structure in the park's battlefield unit. Although referred to by the soldiers of both armies simply as "the white house," the building was home to James and Adeline Shirley and is better known as the Shirley House.

"Judge" Shirley, as James was called by the residents of Vicksburg, had moved to the Hill City in 1836 with his second wife, Adeline, and a son by his previous marriage. Here, he established a lucrative law practice and dealt in real estate and the sale of agricultural produce. As James's fortune grew, so too did his family. Adeline gave birth to a son, Frederick, in 1836. The couple's only daughter, Alice, arrived in 1844. And "Mother's Precious," Robert Quincy, was born in 1848.

To escape the recurring plague of yellow fever that seemed to annually impact Vicksburg, Judge Shirley sought to move his family to a healthier location and on January 1, 1851, purchased Wexford Lodge and 60 acres of land. Although the Shirleys were Northerners, and New Englanders at that, to help with their growing family and work their land they became slave owners. Still, throughout the secession crisis, they remained outspoken supporters of the Federal government. During the war itself, Alice even boldly played patriotic tunes on the piano in the relative quiet of their country home.

But, in the late spring of 1863, war came to their very door, and the Shirleys were forced from their home. During the siege of Vicksburg, Wexford Lodge was at first situated between the opposing lines and riddled by shot and shell. The family's belongings were broken and scattered by soldiers who occupied their home or bivouacked in the yard. Their gardens were destroyed as troops in Union blue excavated approaches toward the Confederate works. The house was so badly damaged that the Shirleys never returned to their once-happy home.

Vicksburg was a young community when Nicholas Gray moved there. A native of Wexford County, Ireland, Gray was a picturesque and adventuresome figure. Arrested for his participation in the Irish Rebellion, he was imprisoned from 1803 to 1806. Upon his release, he decided to leave Ireland and seek his fortune elsewhere. He came to America around 1808 and settled in New York City. In 1815, the Irishman was named register of the land office of the Mississippi Territory and settled in Washington, Adams County. He later moved to Vicksburg in the 1830s and on August 1, 1837, purchased a tract of land from T.H. Goodall. There, he built the home he called Wexford Lodge. Pictured just prior to the Civil War, Wexford Lodge was situated along Jackson Road east of Vicksburg and was described as "a most desirable residence in a healthy location."

James Shirley was a native of Goffstown, New Hampshire, and an 1818 graduate of Dartmouth College. A lawyer by training who first practiced in Albany, New York, James later assumed charge of an academy in Georgia. Following the death of his wife, he moved first to Alabama, then to Mississippi. During the course of his travels, he met and married Adeline Quincy of Boston, Massachusetts.

This is Alice Eugenia Shirley as she appeared at the time of the Civil War. Her father boasted, "Alice is the best scholar of her age I have ever seen. Learns herself with little or no assistance, is a healthy fine looking girl very active and spritely in mind and body." During the siege, she met Union chaplain John Eaton of Ohio, whom she later married.

The Shirley House during the siege in 1863 was surrounded by "shebangs," or dugouts, excavated by members of the 45th Illinois Infantry to escape the fire of Confederate sharpshooters and heat of a Mississippi summer. Directly in front of the house is Logan's Approach, which was excavated by Union soldiers who, with pick and shovel, dug their way to the Third Louisiana Redan, which guarded the Jackson Road entry into Vicksburg.

Shortly after the establishment of the park, Captain Rigby of the park commission initiated efforts to purchase the building and grounds from Alice Shirley Eaton to restore the house and open it as a war memorial. Alice agreed to the sale provided that the house be restored so that it was the "most conspicuous object" in the park. She made another stipulation: "I would like to bury by the old house, my father and mother, whom the war drove from it." In partial fulfillment of Alice's demands and to demonstrate the government's good will, before the sale was consummated Captain Rigby had the remains of James and Adeline Shirley disinterred from Vicksburg's Cedar Hill Cemetery and reinterred behind the house. Abandoned for decades, the Shirley House stood in ruin in the 1890s when veterans began their effort to create a national military park.

Alice described her house as being "built after the southern fashion, a story and a half in height, a wide hall in center, large rooms on each side, ceilings high, upper and lower porch in front, and veranda in the rear. It stood on an elevation somewhat back from the [Jackson] road. A driveway describing a semi-circle passed the door, and a wide walk ran from the front porch to the road, which was reached from that point by a flight of steps." The west side of the Shirley House is shown before and after restoration in 1902.

The garden, which Alice noted was "my father's special pride," was located behind the house. Alice recalled, "To old Uncle Will, the oldest slave on the place, tall, bent, black, and wrinkled, was given the care of this garden." Through his labors, she said, the garden "kept us so bountifully supplied with vegetables and small fruits and also boasted of one row of peanut hills." Alice recorded, "The kitchen and four other buildings where the servants slept were on either side of the gardens and they were all quite comfortable, had good fireplaces and plank floors." The back of the Shirley House is shown here before and after restoration in 1902.

Although they were driven from their home by war, the spirit of the family was never broken. Alice remembered, "The Fourth of July, 1863, was a day of great joy to my father. Half sick and worn out with the long strain, his horses and carriages and servants gone, his home a wreck; yet he was a proud and happy man to be able to walk into town under the old flag, the bands playing the National airs, and the Stars and Stripes waving from the Court house." The east side of the Shirley House is pictured before and after restoration in 1902.

Restored to its former glory, as Alice had insisted upon, "the white house" is the "most conspicuous object" in the park. The Shirley House is seen here from Logan Tower, which stood on the opposite side of Jackson Road and east of the house. Wexford Lodge is seen as it appeared in 1908 shortly after dedication of the Illinois Monument, which stands at left.

By executive order of Pres. Franklin Roosevelt, the national military park was transferred from the War Department to the Department of the Interior in 1933. Since that date, the park has been administered by the National Park Service, which initially established its headquarters in the Shirley House. The Shirley House is seen here as it appeared in the 1930s when it served as park headquarters and residence of the park superintendent.

To provide better views of the battlefield, three observation towers were constructed between 1907 and 1910. The first tower was along Jackson Road at "Logan Circle," which was located east of the Shirley House. A second tower went up on Confederate Avenue, east of Fort Hill. And the third was along Confederate Avenue near All Saints School. Although a favorite feature with park visitors, all three were removed in the 1960s.

The Willis-Cowan House on Crawford Street in Vicksburg was the headquarters of Confederate general John C. Pemberton from May 23 to July 4, 1863, and is the building in which the decision was made to surrender the city. Although veterans desired it to be included in the park, acquisition was excluded from the enabling act. In 2002, Pres. George W. Bush signed legislation authorizing its acquisition by the National Park Service.

In 1937, shortly after the park was transferred from the War Department to the Department of the Interior, the National Park Service opened its administration building/museum on Pemberton Avenue opposite the Surrender Interview Site. As it was not situated along the designated tour route, few people visited. Following World War II, the building was converted to a residence for the park superintendent.

After World War II, the park's administrative offices and museum were moved to a larger building situated closer to the park entrance, near present-day Tour Stop 12. This facility served as the park's Visitor Center until 1971, when the current Visitor Center opened. The old white building was removed in 1973.

In order to upgrade the national parks in time for the agency's 50th anniversary in 1966, Pres. Dwight Eisenhower initiated the Mission 66 program. Among the improvements made at Vicksburg was construction of one of the city's major transportation arteries, Mission 66, in order to remove local traffic from the park tour road. The current Visitor Center was also constructed, though it was not opened until 1971.

Six

Illinois Monument

Approximately 36,325 soldiers from Illinois participated in the Vicksburg campaign, making up one half of the Union Army of the Tennessee, which was commanded by Maj. Gen. Ulysses S. Grant. That number also represents almost 30 percent of all troops engaged in the campaign in the armies of the North and South. As Vicksburg was the most decisive campaign of the Civil War, and as Illinois troops played such a prominent role in gaining Union victory, it is only fitting that Illinois erected a monument the grandeur of which the people of the Sucker State will always be justly proud.

On May 11, 1901, in response to urging by the state's veterans, the general assembly in Springfield passed a bill creating a commission to ascertain and mark the positions occupied by Illinois troops in the Siege of Vicksburg. The act also appropriated $2,000 for the work of the commission. (There was $4.79 left when the work was finished.) On July 1, pursuant to that act, Gov. Richard Yates Jr. appointed 18 members to serve on the commission, all of whom were veterans of the Vicksburg campaign.

The duly appointed commissioners met in Chicago on November 23, 1901, and formally organized by electing John C. Black (formerly of the 37th Illinois Infantry) president, Asa C. Matthews (who had served in the 99th Infantry) vice president, George S. Durfee (late of the 8th Infantry) secretary, and Charles Koch (a former member of the 72nd Infantry) assistant secretary and treasurer.

The following spring, the commissioners traveled to Vicksburg via Chattanooga and spent six days in the park to do the necessary fieldwork in determining the positions of Illinois commands during the siege. Numbered stakes were driven into the ground at each location and the positions recorded by the park's resident commissioner, Captain Rigby.

Upon completion of their work, the commissioners reported to Governor Yates, "Illinois is justly proud of the achievements of her patriotic sons. Every heart-beat of her generous people vibrates with praise for the valor, courage, fidelity and victories of her 'men at arms.' "

Gov. Richard Yates, at left, son of Illionois's wartime governor, captured the heart and soul of this endeavor as he expressed, "The building of durable and appropriate monuments to mark the places where brave men have struggled and fallen on the line of duty in defense of their country and its institutions, is not only the highest privilege of patriotism, but the most impressive evidence that succeeding generations appreciate both the value and necessity of heroic deeds." In closing his message, Yates asserted, "I most fervently trust that our generation will not hesitate to offer willing tribute to the noble men who fought and fell, and who by deeds of heroism conquered—not a people, but a peace, which has brought us priceless benedictions." Members of the Illinois-Vicksburg Military Park Commission are pictured below with the park commissioners assembled in front of the Shirley House on December 13, 1904, for ground-breaking ceremonies. (MDAH.)

On May 14, 1903, an act of the general assembly in Springfield created the Illinois-Vicksburg Military Park Commission—comprised of nine members shown at right, all of whom were veterans of the Vicksburg campaign—and appropriated the requested amount of $250,000. John C. Black was again elected president. Because of poor health, however, he resigned in December 1903 and was replaced by Asa C. Matthews. The commission organized in Springfield on August 6, 1903, and bylaws were adopted at a meeting held in Chicago on August 18. The executive committee consisted of Matthews, Charles Koch, George Durfee, Francis Riddle (formerly of the 130th Infantry), and Harvey Trimble. Below, the Illinois commissioners are pictured breaking ground for the Illinois Monument on December 13, 1904.

William L.B. Jenney, at left, who had served as Gen. William T. Sherman's chief engineer during the siege of Vicksburg, was selected as artist and architect. On December 15, 1903, the Chicago firm of Jenney & Mundie was employed as architects, and they entered into a contract in which they agreed to furnish all the necessary plans, drawings, and specifications for the state monument and regimental markers. Three months later, on March 12, 1904, the plans and specifications were adopted by the commission, and letters of invitation were sent out to bidders; 61 applications for the plans were received. The commission met in Springfield on May 23 and opened the bids. To their great disappointment, only five proposals were received, of which only one fell within the amount of the appropriated funds. A contract was thus awarded to the Culver Construction Company of Springfield, Illinois, to furnish all materials and work for the erection of the monument. Below, the construction crew is shown as it begins work on January 1, 1905.

Mules, men, and machines work together to construct the Illinois Monument. Here, preparations are made to pour the base of the monument. A small tent city, a portion of which can be seen at right, housed the workers who lived on site throughout the construction project. The dog at left was the pet of J.S. Culver, who oversaw construction of the monument.

Italian craftspeople place the first stone on April 8, 1905. The massive granite slabs and blocks had been quarried and cut elsewhere and sent to Vicksburg by rail. Once the stone was hoisted and positioned, the craftspeople trimmed and shimmed the stone for proper alignment.

Work continued over the next 15 months, during which time members of the Illinois Commission made several trips to Vicksburg to inspect the progress on the monument. William T. Rigby, chairman of the park commission (seated fourth from right, with cigar in his left hand), hosts members of the Illinois legislature in the Shirley House in March 1905. (MDAH.)

The monument is taking shape on June 1, 1905; the steps and base of the temple are made of Stone Mountain granite, while the main body is constructed of Georgia marble. There are 47 steps leading from Jackson Road to the rotunda—one step for each day of the siege of Vicksburg.

In this image from September 1, 1905, the rotunda is taking shape, and one of the six Doric monolith columns is being hoisted into place. The monument, which may look familiar, is patterned after the Pantheon in Rome and is approximately one fourth the size of that famous temple.

Work on the portico began on November 1, 1905, as did work on the canopied dome. The portico is 32 feet wide and 14 feet deep. The dome is 62 feet high and has an oculus, or "eye," 11 feet in diameter to provide light and ventilation.

Exterior work on the monument, shown here on April 1, 1906, was completed two weeks later. In addition to its state memorial, Illinois placed 79 regimental monuments and markers, all of which were installed by April 19 and accepted by the commission.

The bronze eagle that graces the portico was sculpted by Frederick Hibbard and weighs one ton. Once emplaced above the portico, it was gilded with a double layer of gold leaf, and a coating of lacquer was applied to maintain its luster. A native of Canton, Missouri, Hibbard also sculpted the equestrian statue of General Grant that stands in the park.

Above the portico are the figures of three women that symbolize the North and South "reunited in peace." Between the columns, from left to right, are relief portraits of Abraham Lincoln, Ulysses. S. Grant, and Illinois's wartime governor Richard Yates. These works were executed by Charles Mulligan.

On December 9, 1905, the full commission again visited Vicksburg and made a thorough inspection of the monument. It was then decided to offset the interior inscriptions with bronze gilding and the bronze eagle that adorned the portico with gold leaf. This work being performed, the state monument was completed by April 15, 1906. Though badly damaged, this photograph shows members of the Illinois-Vicksburg Military Park Commission making final inspection of the monument prior to dedication.

At 8:00 a.m. on Friday, October 26, 1906, the men of the 1st Infantry, Illinois National Guard (800 strong), formed ranks on Monroe Street in the shadow of the historic Warren County Courthouse, where the flag of the 45th Illinois had been raised on July 4, 1863, symbolizing Union victory. Also moving into formation were Companies A, B, and F of the 3rd Infantry, Mississippi National Guard, and hundreds of dignitaries, guests, and veterans of the Blue and Gray in carriages and on horseback. Moving through the streets of Vicksburg, which were decorated with red, white, and blue bunting, a vast crowd of citizens followed along the parade route. After marching two miles, the parade entered the grounds of the national military park, and the governor's salute was fired by the Warren Light Artillery, Battery E, of the Mississippi National Guard. Pictured here on dedication day are the officers of the 1st Regiment Infantry, Illinois National Guard, leading the parade along Grove Street to the park.

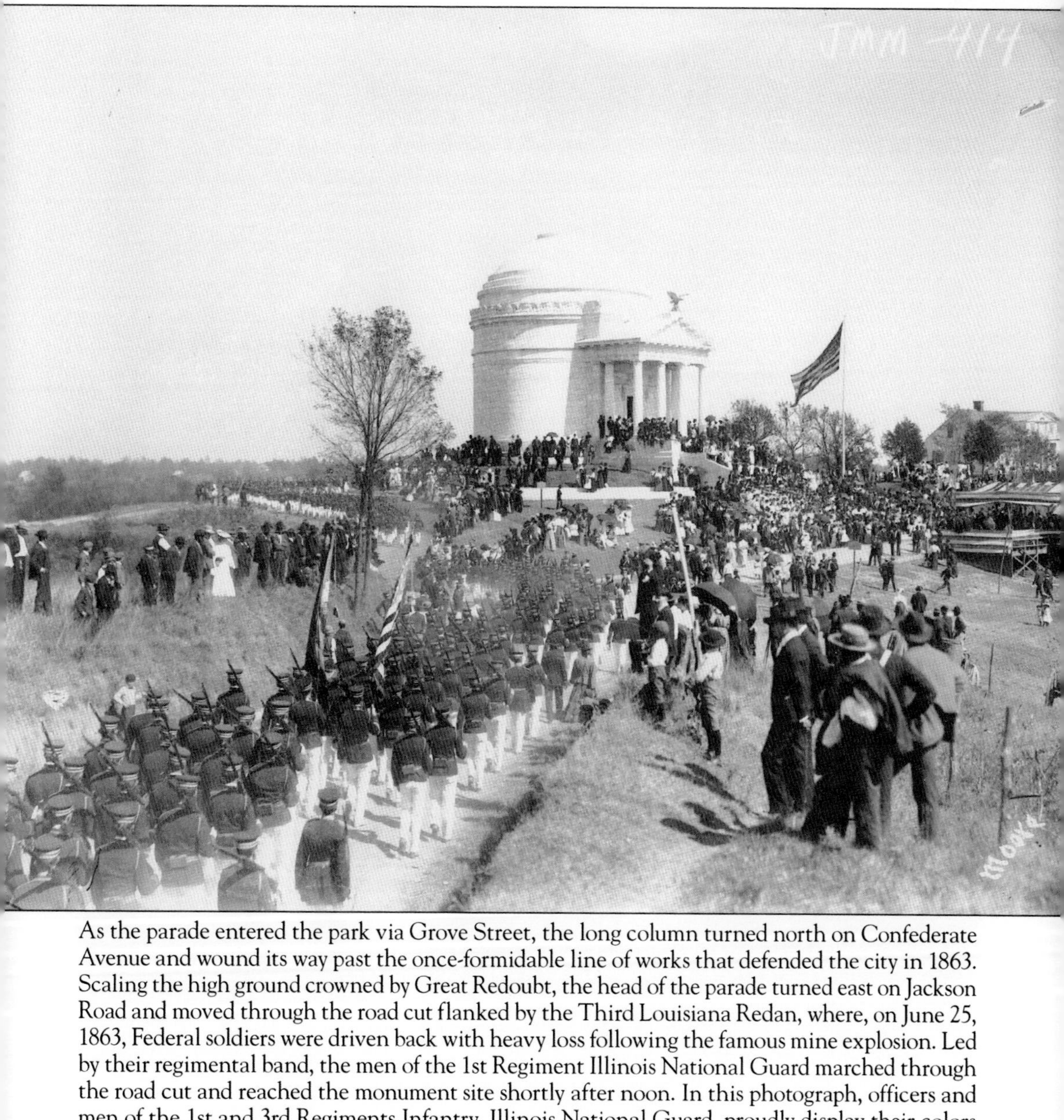

As the parade entered the park via Grove Street, the long column turned north on Confederate Avenue and wound its way past the once-formidable line of works that defended the city in 1863. Scaling the high ground crowned by Great Redoubt, the head of the parade turned east on Jackson Road and moved through the road cut flanked by the Third Louisiana Redan, where, on June 25, 1863, Federal soldiers were driven back with heavy loss following the famous mine explosion. Led by their regimental band, the men of the 1st Regiment Illinois National Guard marched through the road cut and reached the monument site shortly after noon. In this photograph, officers and men of the 1st and 3rd Regiments Infantry, Illinois National Guard, proudly display their colors as the long column reaches the dedication site on Jackson Road.

A vast crowd assembled on the steps of the monument to listen to the dedicatory addresses delivered from the speaker's platform at right. Promptly at 12:30 p.m., Colonel Matthews called the assembly to order. The Reverend Alanson R. Morgan raised his hands and asked that the crowd bow their heads in silence. His golden voice then raised to the heavens a solemn prayer to the Almighty.

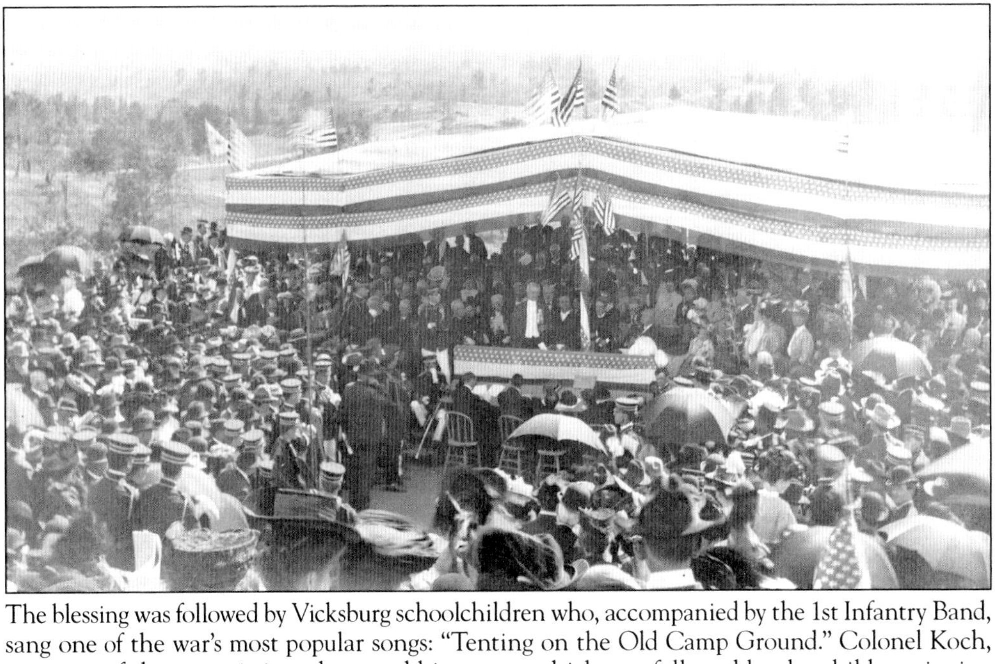

The blessing was followed by Vicksburg schoolchildren who, accompanied by the 1st Infantry Band, sang one of the war's most popular songs: "Tenting on the Old Camp Ground." Colonel Koch, secretary of the commission, then read his report, which was followed by the children singing "Illinois." President Matthews (in white vest) of the Illinois-Vicksburg Military Park Commission then rose to present the monument to Governor Deneen.

Colonel Matthews presented the monument on behalf of the commission to Governor Deneen, along with a key to the temple. Governor Deneen (at right) stood and spoke of mankind's exaltation and admiration of courage and bravery and observed, "These monuments are erected in no narrow spirit. They are the chroniclers neither of victory nor of defeat, but stand as an everlasting testimony to the heroism of the Illinois soldier." Echoing the sentiments expressed by Illinois's favorite son, Abraham Lincoln, in his Gettysburg Address, Deneen closed his remarks by saying, "And to us who are the heirs of the dear-bought but glorious legacy of honor which they have bestowed upon our State and Nation this occasion is fraught with solemn thoughts of gratitude to the dead and living heroes who bequeathed to us this heritage of freedom and of union, and of the obligation which is ours to hand it down, unsullied and unimpaired, and made more glorious with the passing years, to our posterity." He then presented the monument to the US government.

In addition to the speech made by Illinois governor Charles Deneen, addresses were also given by Governors Newton Blanchard of Louisiana and James K. Vardaman of Mississippi. The monument was accepted on behalf of the government by John C. Scofield (at left), chief clerk of the War Department. The main oration that day was given by ambassador William J. Calhoun (below), who in closing his remarks said, "The spirit of patriotism and its sacrifices, and in honor of the dead, who exemplified that spirit in life and death we dedicate this monument." Following the singing of "The Star-Spangled Banner," the ceremony closed with a benediction by Reverend Morgan.

The Illinois Monument honors the 36,325 soldiers from Illinois who served during the Vicksburg campaign. Half of the Union army that gained victory at Vicksburg came from Illinois. Their names are listed alphabetically by regiment and company on 60 bronze tablets along the interior wall of the monument.

Fred Grant (center), son of Gen. Ulysses S. Grant, visits the Illinois Monument in May 1907. Standing to the right of Grant (with open coat) is former Confederate lieutenant general and park commissioner Stephen D. Lee. Standing at base of flagpole is famed sculptor Henry Hudson Kitson, many of whose works grace the park landscape.

Fred Grant and his wife, Ida, stand on the steps of the Illinois Monument in May 1907. Fred was a veteran of the Vicksburg campaign who, at the age of 12, was wounded during the Battle of Big Black River Bridge on May 17, 1863. He had been instrumental in the establishment of the park and was a frequent and popular visitor to Vicksburg.

Seven

State Monuments and Statuary

The park's enabling act provides "that it shall be lawful for any State that had troops engaged in the siege and defense of Vicksburg to enter upon the lands of the Vicksburg national military park for the purpose of ascertaining and marking the lines of battle of its troops engaged therein." Thus, it is a state responsibility to erect monuments.

As Vicksburg was a significant Union victory, perhaps the most decisive of the Civil War, the Northern states were quick to appropriate generous sums of money for monuments at the site. Conversely, the Southern states were loath to follow suit; after all, Vicksburg had been a stunning and disastrous Confederate defeat. Compounding reluctance, the Southern states were still in an economic depression caused by the war and the Reconstruction period that followed. Besides, a number of Southern legislators refused to appropriate money for monuments in what was termed by many a "Yankee park." But, in time, each of the Southern states placed monuments at Vicksburg.

During his tenure as resident commissioner and then chairman of the park commission, Captain Rigby labored tirelessly to make Vicksburg the finest of the nation's military parks. In honoring the men who struggled at Vicksburg in the spring and summer of 1863, he worked with state commissions, veterans' organizations, and a host of individuals to secure placement of state memorials, regimental monuments and markers, and bronze and stone statuary that range from equestrian statues and standing figures to busts and relief portraits that were executed by the foremost American and European sculptors of the late 19th and early 20th centuries. Thanks largely to his efforts, Vicksburg National Military Park today boasts of approximately 1,380 monuments, markers, tablets, and plaques, making it one of the more densely monumented battlefields in the world. Collectively, they have made Vicksburg, in the words of one Civil War veteran, "The art park of the world."

The Commonwealth of Massachusetts was the first state to place and dedicate a memorial to its soldiers who served in the Vicksburg campaign. Here, 10 yoke of oxen draw the 15-ton boulder that serves as the base of the Massachusetts Monument along Jackson Street, past its intersection with Adams Street, in 1903.

Soldiers of the 29th, 35th, and 36th Massachusetts Infantry Regiments, attached to the IX Corps, represented the Bay State during the Vicksburg campaign. Gov. John L. Bates of Massachusetts delivers the main oration at dedication of the Massachusetts Monument on November 14, 1903.

The Massachusetts soldiers of the IX Corps were positioned north of Vicksburg, near Milldale, to prevent Confederate relief forces from approaching along the Mechanicsburg Corridor. On November 14, 1903, schoolgirls from Vicksburg provided "vocal music" during the dedication of the Massachusetts Monument.

Titled *The Volunteer*, the Massachusetts Monument is the work of sculptress Theo Alice Ruggles Kitson. The boulder that serves as the base came from Massachusetts, as did the scattered rocks, which symbolize the rugged terrain over which these soldiers fought while in Mississippi.

Theo Alice Ruggles Kitson has 73 pieces of bronze dotting the park landscape, making her the most prolific of the Vicksburg artists. A native of Brookline, Massachusetts, born in 1871, she studied sculpting in New York under the celebrated Henry Kitson, whom she married in 1893.

Henry Kitson was among the most renowned sculptors of the late 19th and early 20th centuries. Born in 1865 and a native of Huddersfield, England, Kitson immigrated to America in 1876 and established a studio in Boston. Many of the bronze works at Vicksburg that were executed by the Kitsons were cast at the Tiffany Studio.

Dedication of the Pennsylvania Monument, planned for 1905, was postponed a year because of a yellow fever epidemic in Vicksburg. Standing at left under the canopy, Park commissioner William T. Rigby (right) and former Union general Samuel K. Schwenk, chairman of the Vicksburg Battlefield Commission of Pennsylvania, get set to start the ceremony to dedicate the Pennsylvania Monument on March 24, 1906.

Pennsylvania governor Samuel Pennypacker and Mississippi governor James K. Vardaman (second and third to the left, respectively, of the woman in the white blouse) stand at the start of the ceremony. Vardaman, who addressed the crowd that day, was reportedly "fully up to the standard of that well known orator of whom Mississippi is proud."

Anna Mai Schwenk, niece of General Schwenk, recites a poem titled "Roll Back the Years" that was written for the occasion by Jack Crawford, the "Poet Scout." Crawford is the man with long hair sitting directly behind Anna Mai.

Gov. Samuel Pennypacker (standing at left center) delivers a short address as he accepts the monument on behalf of the Commonwealth of Pennsylvania and in turn presents it to the US government. John Scofield, chief clerk of the War Department, accepted the monument on behalf of Secretary of War William Howard Taft.

The shaft of the Pennsylvania Monument is draped with US flags as the dedication ceremonies proceed under the canopy at left. The flags, which measured 12 feet by 24 feet each, were provided by the Signal Corps of the Illinois National Guard.

The Pennsylvania Monument is unveiled following the main oration by former Pennsylvania governor James A. Beaver. Lillian Von Schwenk (another niece of General Schwenk) and Laura Campbell unveiled the monument, and the flags were hoisted up the poles that flanked the memorial.

Union veterans from the Commonwealth of Pennsylvania who had participated in the Vicksburg campaign pose in front of the newly dedicated monument on March 24, 1906, along with members of the 3rd Infantry, Mississippi National Guard.

The Pennsylvania Monument, designed by Albert Randolph Ross, is an ellipse that features bronze medallions of the commanders of the four regiments of infantry and one battery of artillery from Pennsylvania that participated in the Vicksburg campaign.

The inscription on the Pennsylvania Monument is considered the most beautiful expression on any state monument at Vicksburg. The relief of John I. Curtin is at left. Colonel Curtin, who commanded the 45th Pennsylvania Infantry, was the younger brother of Pennsylvania's war governor, Andrew Gregg Curtin, who is also memorialized with a bronze bust along Pennsylvania Avenue in the park. The middle relief is of John F. Hartranft of the 51st Pennsylvania Infantry, who later commanded the military prison at the Washington Arsenal when the conspirators responsible for the assassination of Abraham Lincoln were imprisoned there in 1865. Hartranft went on to serve as governor of the Commonwealth of Pennsylvania from 1873 to 1879. The relief portraits were executed by Charles Lopez.

The year 1906 was a busy one at the park with monument construction projects and dedication ceremonies. The Pennsylvania Monument was dedicated in March and the Illinois Monument in October. The following month, a large contingent of veterans and dignitaries from Iowa came to dedicate their state memorial. In this photograph, large US flags cover the center portion of the Iowa Monument on dedication day: November 15, 1906.

John F. Merry, considered the "Father of the Vicksburg National Military Park Idea," also served as chairman of the Iowa Monument Commission. As the ceremony is about to begin, Merry is the first man standing to the left of the center pole. Behind him stands Gov. Albert Cummins of Iowa.

The large crowd bows their heads as Rev. Dr. A.L. Frisbie offers the invocation to start the dedication ceremony. "We remember those who fell here. We cannot hallow or consecrate this ground. We can only dedicate to the memory of the brave dead these monuments, which shall testify to their fidelity, their courage, their self-sacrifice, their loyalty to the principles in which they believed."

Gov. Albert Cummins (in white vest) of Iowa presents the Iowa Monument to the US government. Cummins, a Pennsylvania native who later practiced law in Des Moines, became the 18th governor of Iowa in 1902 and served three successive terms. He later was a US senator and twice sought the Republican nomination for president. On his swing through the South, Cummins dedicated Iowa monuments at Vicksburg, Chattanooga, Shiloh, and Andersonville.

The Iowa Monument features six bas-reliefs that depict the actions of Iowa soldiers and sailors in the Vicksburg campaign. Sculpted by renowned artist Henry Hudson Kitson, this relief features the 17th Iowa Infantry Regiment advancing on the Jackson, Mississippi, capital city, on May 14, 1863.

Although dedicated in 1906, the large equestrian statue was added in 1912 and symbolizes the indomitable spirit of the American soldier. This magnificent sculpture is the work of Henry Kitson and Theo Alice Ruggles Kitson. The Kitsons, who married in 1893, were estranged by this time but collaborated to do this work.

Park commissioner William Rigby plays host to the Indiana delegation in December 1908. The group, led by former Union general George McGinnis (center, with hat and paper in hand), poses for this photograph at the base of the Indian Mound in Vicksburg National Cemetery. Note the original wooden gazebo and the decorative capstones on the staircase.

On December 29, 1908, the State of Indiana formally dedicated its regimental monuments. (The state monument would be placed and dedicated in 1926.) Park commissioner Rigby, sitting left of the center pole, listens attentively. Former Union general George McGinnis of Indiana is second to the left of Rigby.

The host state, Mississippi, had originally planned to dedicate its monument in 1907, but the bronze components were not then finished. Although still not completed by 1909, the Mississippi commissioners set November 13, 1909, as dedication day. The band of the Volunteer Southrons, a local militia unit, leads the parade of veterans and dignitaries from town to the dedication site along Confederate Avenue.

In January 1906, when a bill was introduced in the state legislature in Jackson to establish a monument commission, it met with stiff opposition. A number of Confederate veterans were members of the legislature, and they believed that it would be disgraceful for Mississippi to erect a memorial in what one legislator termed a "Yankee park." In this image, the incomplete monument towers above the crowd listening to the dedicatory addresses.

Thanks to the efforts of the charismatic Stephen D. Lee, who lobbied hard on behalf of the monument, both the authorization bill to establish a Mississippi-Vicksburg Monument Commission and the appropriation measure passed by just one vote. Here, the large crowd that assembled for dedication of the Mississippi Monument poses for Vicksburg photographer J. Mack Moore.

In this photograph taken in 1911, scaffolding is being removed from the recently completed Wisconsin Monument, and the site is being prepared for dedication day that was set for May 22, 1911. On bronze tablets that line the plaza are the names of more than 9,000 soldiers from Wisconsin who participated in the Vicksburg campaign.

Florence F. Weissert (in white dress at bottom of shaft), daughter of August G. Weissert, secretary of the Wisconsin-Vicksburg Commission, stands ready to unveil the monument while the crowd listens attentively to the address being delivered from beneath the canopy at right by Wisconsin governor Francis McGovern. Note the horse-drawn concession wagon at left, where those in attendance could purchase "mothers made cream, pop corn, and hot peanuts."

Maj. Gen. Frederick D. Grant, son of the Union commander at Vicksburg, Maj. Gen. Ulysses S. Grant, is flanked by Gov. Francis McGovern of Wisconsin (right) and Gov. Edmund F. Noel of Mississippi (left). At the age of 12, Fred Grant was wounded during the Vicksburg campaign in the Battle of Big Black River Bridge.

Components of the Wisconsin Monument include bronze reliefs portraits honoring Wisconsin sailors on duty in the federal navy during the Vicksburg campaign and soldiers who served in the artillery branch of the army. The relief portrait on the back of the monument features soldiers of both armies reunited as brothers, their reunion being blessed by the Angel of Peace.

The most conspicuous feature of the Wisconsin Monument is the bronze likeness of Old Abe, the war eagle of the 8th Wisconsin Infantry, which crowns the 57-foot-high shaft. There are 33 steps leading to the temple floor, which is flanked by bronze figures of a Union cavalryman (left) and soldier standing guard (right).

Named in honor of Pres. Abraham Lincoln, Old Abe was taken into battle tethered to a post in the form of a shield. The war eagle survived 36 engagements and was retired in 1864. Placed on a perch in the Wisconsin capitol, the bird died from smoke inhalation during a fire in 1881. Old Abe is the official mascot of the famous Screaming Eagles of the present-day 101st Airborne Infantry.

Park commissioner Stephen D. Lee (sitting left of center with white goatee) and members of the Louisiana-Vicksburg Battlefield Commission pose on the steps of the Warren County Court House in 1902. Although this commission selected a site for the state monument in 1902, almost 20 years would pass before construction of the Louisiana Monument began. (MDAH.)

Sections of the Louisiana Monument lie scattered on the slope of Great Redoubt as a crane hoists the capstone into position. Louisiana, the first Southern state to select a site for its monument, chose Great Redoubt, which was defended by Louisiana soldiers during the siege. (MDAH.)

Louisiana had more troops in the defense line around Vicksburg than any other Southern state. Among the soldiers from Louisiana who served in the campaign was Capt. David Todd, brother-in-law of Abraham Lincoln. This view shows the state seal at the base of the monument, which features a brown pelican feeding her three chicks with the words "Union, Justice, Confidence" inscribed around them. (MDAH.)

The 81-foot-tall Doric column stands atop the highest point in Warren County (397 feet above sea level) and towers above Great Redoubt. Constructed of Stone Mountain granite, the Louisiana Monument was dedicated on October 18, 1920. The flaming brazier that crowns the shaft symbolizes eternal peace. (MDAH.)

A delegation of Union veterans from West Virginia prepares to leave Charleston en route to Vicksburg for the dedication of the West Virginia Monument. In the center in a light gray suit is H.S. White, chairman of the West Virginia–Vicksburg Park Commission. Standing in front of him, dressed as a Union soldier, is his grandson. (MDAH.)

These Vicksburg schoolgirls, standing in front of the flag-draped monument, provided song during the dedication ceremony on November 12, 1922. The Mountain State was represented by only one unit during the Vicksburg campaign: the 4th West Virginia Volunteer Infantry. The unit was originally commanded by Joseph A.J. Lightburn, who commanded a brigade during the campaign and whose relief portrait is located on Graveyard Road, a few yards beyond the state memorial.

The West Virginia Monument features a bronze bust of Maj. Arza Goodspeed of the 4th West Virginia Infantry, who was killed in the May 19, 1863, assault against Vicksburg. Goodspeed was a native of Athens, Ohio, and a graduate of Ohio University. He enlisted as a private in the 3rd Ohio Infantry and was later commissioned an officer in the 4th West Virginia.

Park commissioner Rigby (fourth from right) and members of the West Virginia commission are seen here shortly after dedication of the state monument. H.S. White (in the light suit), chairman of the delegation, and his wife are standing directly in front of the monument. Between them is R.O. Sears, the builder of the monument. The sculptor was Aristide Berto Cianfarani.

During Lee's last visit to Vicksburg, Captain Rigby had the general pose for a photograph on the spot from which he had witnessed the May 22, 1863, assault against his lines. The photograph taken that day was the basis for this monument that was sculpted by the renowned Henry Kitson. Although Rigby desired to have the monument dedicated in Lee's lifetime, the general died shortly after the photograph was taken. The statue was dedicated on June 11, 1909. Pictured below on that day is Lee's son Blewett (third from left, with hat in hand) and Blewett's son John Glessner Lee (with flag over his shoulder). The general's nephew Lee Harrison is at far left.

Here are clay models of the equestrian statue honoring Union general Ulysses S. Grant and the standing statue that honors Confederate general John C. Pemberton. The State of Illinois secured the services of Fred Hibbard to execute the work on the Grant form that was cast at the Florentine Brotherhood Foundry in Chicago. Dedicated in 1919, this monument stands on the site of his headquarters during the siege. Sculptor Edmond Quinn was selected by the park commission to produce the monument honoring the Confederate commander. Dedicated in 1917, it stands in the center of the Confederate defense line around Vicksburg.

Eight

National Memorial Celebration and Peace Jubilee

"In commemoration of a half century of peace and good fellowship which happily exist throughout the Republic," Pres. Woodrow Wilson signed legislation on September 8, 1916, authorizing the National Memorial Celebration and Peace Jubilee. For the celebration that would be held on the grounds of the national military park at Vicksburg in October 1917, Congress appropriated $150,000.

Col. Willard D. Newbill of the US Army Quartermaster Corps was assigned the task of supervising the event. He arrived in Vicksburg on March 26, 1917, from Nogales, Arizona, and established his office in the post office building on the corner of Walnut and Crawford Streets of what is today the headquarters of the Lower Mississippi Valley Division of the Corps of Engineers. Assisting Newbill were Col. George Hoskins and 1,250 men of the 155th Infantry (1st Mississippi) who arrived on October 1.

The site selected for the encampment was located in the center of the former siege and defense lines around Vicksburg on what is referred to as the South Loop. "The topography lent unusual artistic effect to the site," reported Newbill, "which was carefully surveyed, mapped and designed." Work on preparing the encampment site was begun on August 8 and completed two months later. This included the construction of roads, installation of water systems and latrines, establishment of hospital facilities, running of electric and telephone lines, stringing of lights, and erection of a massive tent city to accommodate between 18,000 and 20,000 people. Counted among this number were the expected veterans, army personnel assigned to conduct general operations, dignitaries, press corps, and hundreds of support personnel. A 1,000-foot platform was constructed adjacent to the tracks of the Alabama & Vicksburg Railroad (the wartime Southern Railroad of Mississippi) to receive the special trains on which the veterans would arrive. Even an amphitheater, large enough to seat 3,000 people, was constructed; there, speeches would be delivered and silent films shown for the entertainment of those in attendance.

The great event was the largest reunion ever held on the grounds of Vicksburg National Military Park.

A massive tent city was erected by the Quartermaster Corps to accommodate the approximately 8,000 veterans of the Blue and Gray who attend the National Peace Jubilee in October 1917. The tents in the foreground included a post office, press tent, linen tents, a large writing tent where stationary was provided, and other support facilities. In the center is Mess B, and beyond it is the amphitheater.

Field Hospital Company 3 and Ambulance Company 3, US Army, arrived on October 8 from Fort Oglethorpe, Georgia, to provide medical services for those attending the grand reunion. The large tent hospital facility is seen in the rear of the military cantonment area for the soldiers of the 155th Infantry.

As the United States had recently declared war against the Kaiser's Germany and was mobilizing its armed forces for conflict in Europe, military tentage was difficult to obtain. The large tents shown here were provided by the Barnum & Bailey Circus. The open flaps provide a view of the cots on which the veterans slept. Also visible in the center of the photograph is the 60-foot-tall flagpole from which Old Glory flew daily. The reunion opened at sunrise on Tuesday, October 16, with the firing of a signal gun and the raising of the flag. Reveille was followed by an invocation and the singing of "America." That morning, veterans feasted on a breakfast of corn flakes and milk, scrambled eggs with chopped bacon, bread, butter, syrup, and coffee or tea. Note the Illinois Monument, which is also visible above the tree line at left.

Two large mess areas were established to feed the veterans, each were equipped to feed 10,000 men, three meals a day, in separate sittings of 2,100 men each. The meals were prepared by chefs from the famous Grunwald Hotel in New Orleans. Shown here is the kitchen for Mess B. The sign at left, leaning vertically, states, "Tipping prohibited."

Assisting the chefs were nine day cooks and eight night cooks. There were also two butchers, one assigned to each mess. Featured here is the eating area of Mess B, which is set for the noonday meal. The noon meal was the big meal of the day and offered roast beef, pork, or mutton, corn, peas, and dessert.

African American stewards walk among and bus the tables while serving coffee or tea to the veterans. There were 11 headwaiters and 136 regular waiters. An all-black orchestra, the Big Six from Greenville, Mississippi, which provided music during the encampment, also served as waiters when needed.

Supper, or the evening meal, was a light serving that consisted of prunes, pork and beans, rice and gravy, and "Old Dixie Sweets." For men who during the war had eaten a steady diet of hardtack, salt pork, and coffee, the meals at the reunion were truly delectable.

A mule-drawn water wagon helps keep down the dust on the reunion grounds. To the left of the wagon, a truck delivers Coca-Cola. The popular beverage was first bottled in Vicksburg in 1894. At left, veterans enjoy a cool sip of water from one of the many water fountains set up to help soothe parched throats.

The crowd at left gathers around the press tent to hear the latest news on the war in Europe. The post office tent stands at right. Nearby is a tent in which 12 barbers were continually in action from 6:00 a.m. to 6:00 p.m. According to Colonel Newbill, they "did some fine execution upon beards long untouched."

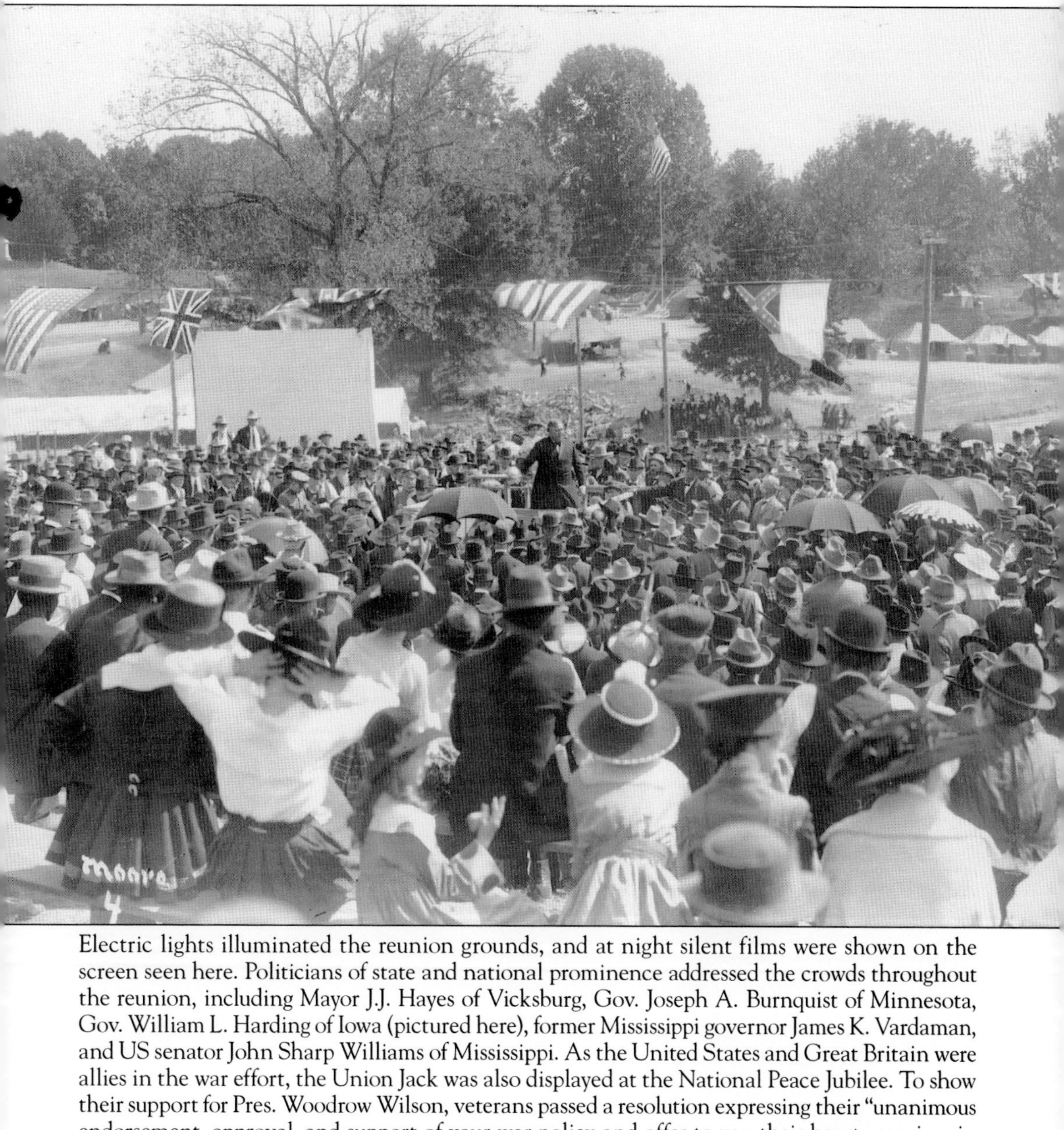

Electric lights illuminated the reunion grounds, and at night silent films were shown on the screen seen here. Politicians of state and national prominence addressed the crowds throughout the reunion, including Mayor J.J. Hayes of Vicksburg, Gov. Joseph A. Burnquist of Minnesota, Gov. William L. Harding of Iowa (pictured here), former Mississippi governor James K. Vardaman, and US senator John Sharp Williams of Mississippi. As the United States and Great Britain were allies in the war effort, the Union Jack was also displayed at the National Peace Jubilee. To show their support for Pres. Woodrow Wilson, veterans passed a resolution expressing their "unanimous endorsement, approval, and support of your war policy and offer to you their hearty services in any capacity that the situation might require." The president responded by telegraph saying that he "would not hesitate to call upon them should the need arise."

Chairman Rigby asked for and received permission to use the funding left over from the reunion, approximately $35,000, to erect a fitting monument in commemoration of the "peace and good fellowship" that prevailed throughout the encampment. His efforts resulted in erection of the Memorial Arch, the inscription on which reads, "Memorial to the National Reunion of Union and Confederate Veterans of the Civil War Oct. 16–19, 1917." The Memorial Arch is gaily bedecked for its dedication on October 20, 1920.

The crowd inspects the newly dedicated Memorial Arch. The smaller stones on either side of the arch list the states of the North and South, in alphabetical order, that were represented by troops during the Vicksburg campaign. Soldiers from 28 states participated in the campaign, siege, and defense of Vicksburg.

Nine

Civilian Conservation Corps

In 1929, William T. Rigby passed away, and the vision and guiding hand of Civil War veterans in management of the park were replaced by members of the Regular Army. Col. Lewis J. Heider was named acting superintendent of the park until a permanent replacement for Rigby was named by the secretary of war. That replacement arrived in 1931 in the person of Maj. John B. Holt, who established the park office as well as his private residence in the Shirley House. Holt's tenure, however, was short lived; in 1933, administration of the park was transferred from the War Department to the National Park Service of the Department of the Interior, which named J. Walter Coleman superintendent.

As Holt labored to continue the work of his predecessors, he struggled to combat the harmful effects of erosion. The nation too struggled with its own difficulties, caught in the grips of the Great Depression. In order to put the nation's labor force back to work, Pres. Franklin D. Roosevelt created the Civilian Conservation Corps, or CCC, in 1933. Four camps of the CCC were established at Vicksburg, each of which became home to 200 enrollees who were supervised by members of the US Army. Wooden barracks were constructed along with a mess hall, recreation hall, education building, motor pool, and other support facilities at each of the four camps.

For a period of almost 10 years, CCC enrollees, who served a six-month tour of duty, sculpted the hillsides to remove the scars of erosion. They also hand-planted the dense forest that now covers most of the park landscape, leaving only a few select vistas to enable visitors to see between the opposing lines occupied by Union and Confederate soldiers. Their work proved invaluable to the sustainability of the park and its infrastructure.

Four camps were established in the park. The first, MP (Military Park)-1, opened in June 1933 and was located along Baldwin's Ferry Road near the entrance to the park. Initially, the camps were massive tent cities; these were eventually replaced with wooden barracks and support facilities.

Enrollees, such as those pictured here, were unmarried men between the ages of 18 and 25. The men of Company 469 who initially occupied MP-1 were mostly Mississippians. The large building to the right of the statue of Col. William Vilas is where the present-day Visitor Center stands.

Enrollees dressed in military-style uniforms and received rudimentary training that served them well during World War II. In addition to the array of conservation projects they performed, there were a number of other activities in which the men could participate. Company 469 at MP-1 was noted for its basketball team that competed against those from other camps.

Enrollees were paid $1 a day. At the end of each month, the men were given $5, and the rest was sent home to their families. During their tour of duty, enrollees received additional education. Those shown here were even trained to serve as the park's first tour guides—a program that continues today.

MP-2, which opened in October 1933, was situated along Confederate Avenue in front of the Louisiana Monument and housed the enrollees of Company 293. Nestled into the natural contours of the land, the slips in which the barracks were constructed are still visible today. Soil erosion–control projects, such as the one shown here, were a primary responsibility of the enrollees in MP-2.

Once the enrollees had eliminated the ugly scars of erosion by sculpting the hillsides, gutters were installed to help channel runoff from the ridgelines to the bottom of ravines and thus help prevent future erosion. Many of the gutters, such as the one shown here being constructed, are still extant and serving the purpose for which they were intended.

MP-3 was constructed along Jackson Road near the observation tower located east of the Shirley House. The men who made up Company 474 formed the camp in June 1934. As with most of the companies that served in Vicksburg, Company 474, which consisted of men from Mississippi and Louisiana, had been organized at Fort McClellan, Alabama, and sent to the park.

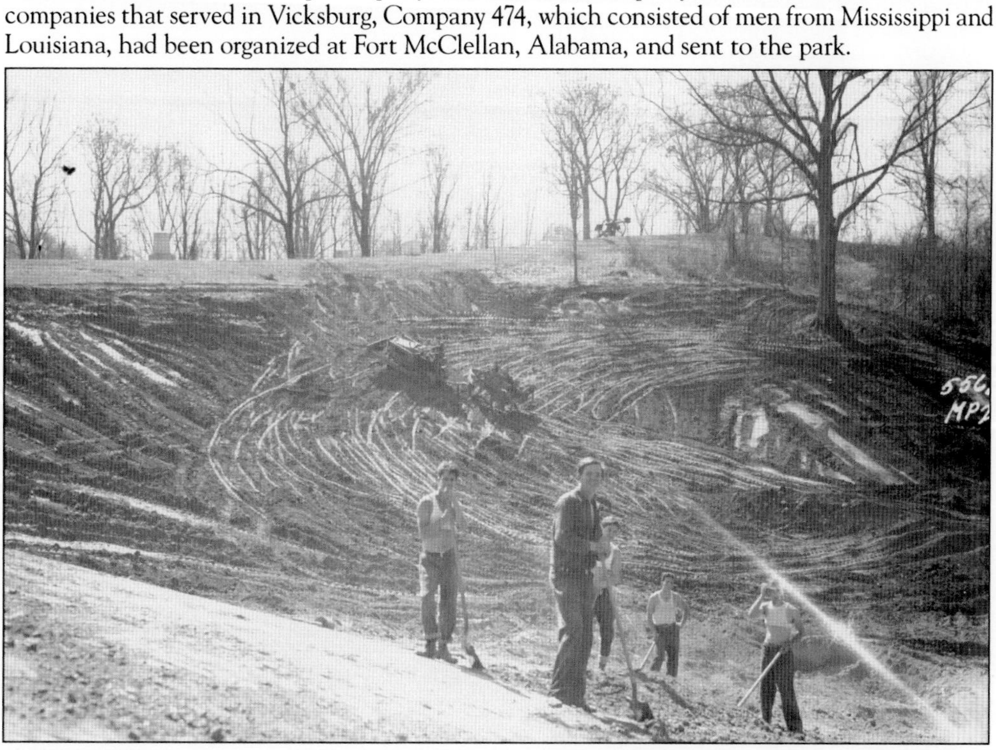

These enrollees of Company 474 performed soil erosion–control projects (as pictured), planted trees, and undertook other park-beautification projects. In their spare time, the enrollees in the camps at Vicksburg organized baseball and basketball teams, played dominoes and checkers, and even formed bands for weekend dances and entertainment.

MP-4, established in May 1934, was located along Union Avenue south of Graveyard Road and was home to the men of Company 1430. Soil erosion–control projects were also the major focus of the enrollees at MP-4. This camp, along with the other three at Vicksburg, was closed by 1942 as the United States entered World War II.

Once the scars of erosion had been removed and the hillsides terraced and sculpted, the enrollees planted trees, which today cover most of the park. Where vistas were established to enable visitors to see between the Union and Confederate positions, sod was planted. Here, enrollees use a unique track-and-cart system to help them sod the steep slopes.

Perhaps the largest and most visible of the soil erosion–control projects completed by the CCC at Vicksburg was at Fort Hill, present-day Tour Stop 9. Fort Hill was the northern anchor of the Confederate defense line around Vicksburg. By 1934, when this photograph was taken from the Indian Mound in the national cemetery, erosion was threatening the historical integrity of this area.

Hundreds of enrollees labored with picks, shovels, and rakes for more than two years to sculpt and terrace the rugged, steep slope of Fort Hill. By 1937, they had completed their task, as shown here. The terrace-and-gutter system they installed is still visible today, but the terraces have lost much of their definition, and the gutters have collapsed in places.

During their years of service at Vicksburg, enrollees uncovered the skeletal remains of several Union and Confederate soldiers. Enrollee Owens is shown here with the remains of a Union soldier he unearthed while working on a soil erosion–control project. CCC enrollees also unearthed and hauled away literal tons of shells, shell fragments, and other Civil War artifacts.

When unearthed, skeletal remains were handled with the utmost dignity and care. In this image, the remains of a Union soldier, uncovered by the CCC, are interred in Vicksburg National Cemetery while enrollees pay their respects. Sadly, all the remains that were reinterred in the national cemetery at Vicksburg are listed in the ledgers simply as "Unknown."

Ten

VICKSBURG NATIONAL CEMETERY

In February 1866, following an inspection tour of the area around Vicksburg, Col. James F. Rushing of the office of the quartermaster general, reported, "Very little had been done here in the way of looking after our dead. Their condition is more deplorable than any post I have visited, while inspector." Throughout west central Mississippi and northeast Louisiana, he found the remains of Union soldiers and sailors "stuck about" and "scattered in shallow graves over wide circuits of the country." In many cases, their bleached bones had been scattered by roaming cattle and hogs. Rushing asked with a tint of shame, "Is not this wrong, not to say hideous, after those brave men have given their lives for the Union?"

In order to provide a proper burial for the men who died in operations focused on the Hill City, the US government purchased 40 acres from Alney Jaynes to establish Vicksburg National Cemetery. Situated on the north side of Mint Spring Bayou, about one and a half miles north of Vicksburg, the land was purchased in August 1866 for the sum of $9,000.

To prepare the site to receive the honored dead, the rugged terrain was terraced, and underground and surface drains were installed. While this work was still in progress, the ghastly process of reinterring the dead began. By 1869, the remains of almost 17,000 Union soldiers and sailors had been moved to Vicksburg for permanent burial. Thus, Vicksburg National Cemetery is the largest national cemetery in the United States in terms of Civil War burials. Sadly, of that number, approximately 13,000 men are unidentified. The graves of those listed simply as "Unknown" are marked by small square blocks.

In accordance with subsequent legislation, veterans of later wars are also interred in the national cemetery, which brings the total number of burials to approximately 18,300. By 1961, all available grave space was either filled or reserved, and so the national cemetery was officially closed.

Completed in 1879, the Arch was the main entrance to the national cemetery. Debris from construction is still visible in the foreground of this photograph. After crossing Glass Bayou at the foot of Cherry Street, the Yazoo City Road (present-day Fort Hill Drive) ran north along the ridge leading to Fort Hill. From there, the National Cemetery Access Road moved down the slope and crossed Mint Spring Bayou via a steel truss bridge and led to the Arch.

This view is looking south along the gravel road leading from the Arch into the cemetery. Fort Hill, the northern anchor of the Confederate defense line around Vicksburg, towers above the Arch, while the site of the powerful water battery is visible beneath the Arch. Floodwaters in the former channel of the Mississippi River can be seen at right.

Pres. William McKinley (who had signed the legislation by which the park was established) enters through the Arch at the southwest corner of the cemetery on May 1, 1901—just four months prior to his assassination in Buffalo. The horses, Frank and Harry, along with the carriage, were furnished by Fisher Funeral Home. The driver is Charles Schuler, while the page sitting next to him is Bernard Fisher.

The entryway was lined with magnolia trees, flowering shrubs, and beds of roses. Approximately 500 magnolias and a number of cedar, holly, and other deciduous and evergreen trees were planted along the drives to provide for evergreen avenues. Vicksburg was among the finest and most beautiful national cemeteries in the system.

The water fountain in Mound E, or "Officer's Circle," in the southwest corner of the cemetery was one of many decorative features of the landscape. Gravity-fed by water from Mint Spring Bayou, the fountain featured a basin that measured 12 feet in diameter. The logjam in the background in the former channel of the Mississippi River was assembled for the nearby Anderson-Tully lumberyard.

"Officer's Circle" is seen here in the early 20th century. By this time, the water fountain was no longer operational, and the catch basin was filled in. Still, the cemetery's beauty and solemnity is captured in this photograph, which shows the beds of roses that lined the entryway. In the foreground are stone blocks that mark the graves of the unidentified in Section J.

A visitor sits on the trunnion of a 10-inch Columbiad. A total of 10 guns placed upright in the ground were scattered throughout the cemetery as ornamentation: seven 32-pounders, two 10-inch Columbiads, and one 9-inch Dahlgren. Over the years, most of the ornamental guns have been removed and either placed on display in the park or transferred to other units of the national park system.

Visitors enjoy the scenic drive over the tree-shaded, gravel loop road through the cemetery. The brick stairs at left provided pedestrian access from the Arch, while the stairs at right enabled visitors to climb the steep terraces. Most of the surface drains visible in this photograph are no longer extant.

This photograph taken from the Indian Mound on Memorial Day 1905 shows the cemetery in all its splendor as tiny US flags decorated the graves of the fallen heroes in Sections I and L. Most of the shrubbery was removed following World War II, and the sharp definition of the terraces has become less defined over the years, but the tradition of placing flags on the graves on Memorial Day continues.

Another view taken on Memorial Day 1905 shows Section V of the cemetery with the Anderson-Tully lumberyard and Vicksburg racetrack in the background. The original wooden headboards were replaced in the 1870s with marble stones; upright stones mark the graves of identified soldiers, whereas small square blocks denote graves of those simply listed as "Unknown."

The rear gate of the national cemetery, often referred to as the center gate, is situated along the Yazoo City Road. The gate has been replaced with a more ornate one and now serves as the main entrance to the cemetery. Note the original cope and capping on the brick enclosure. Also visible above the left gatepost is one the ornamental cannon that was in Mound O.

The rostrum, a common feature in all national cemeteries, was a focal point of activity during funerals, veterans' reunions, and Memorial Day observances. Standing on Sylvan Hill near the flagpole, it had a pergola-style roof that was eventually covered by wisteria vines. Large flowerpots, such as those seen here, were also scattered about the cemetery. The rostrum was also removed after World War II.

The Trindle family graves are found in Section G. John Trindle, a veteran of the 56th Massachusetts Infantry who had lost at leg at Petersburg in 1864, was superintendent of the national cemetery from 1874 until 1882. During his tenure at Vicksburg, he and his wife, Charlotte, lost all four of their children, three of whom died within a few weeks of one another in 1878 as yellow fever swept through the region.

A workman trims the grass around headstones in Section D, while a visitor rests on one of the many benches located throughout the cemetery. The arbor and Surrender Interview Monument stand atop the Indian Mound in the background. The wooden arbor was replaced by the present-day brick rest pavilion in 1931.

Here is another view of the arbor and Surrender Interview Monument looking south across Section L. The large stone monument in the center honors the 25th and 31st Iowa Infantry Regiments, which during the siege of Vicksburg were positioned on this ground. The ornamental cannon near the Iowa monument was removed in 1929, and the site is now the final resting place of Park commissioner William T. Rigby and his wife, Eva Cattron Rigby.

One of the earlier photographs of the burial grounds, looking west toward the Mississippi River, shows the brick enclosure that surrounded the national cemetery. The south wall, at left, has since collapsed and been replaced with a chain-link fence. The historic Yazoo City Road, present-day Connecting Avenue, runs along the east wall of the cemetery in the foreground. The towering eminence of Fort Hill is seen at left.

Discover Thousands of Local History Books Featuring Millions of Vintage Images

Arcadia Publishing, the leading local history publisher in the United States, is committed to making history accessible and meaningful through publishing books that celebrate and preserve the heritage of America's people and places.

Find more books like this at
www.arcadiapublishing.com

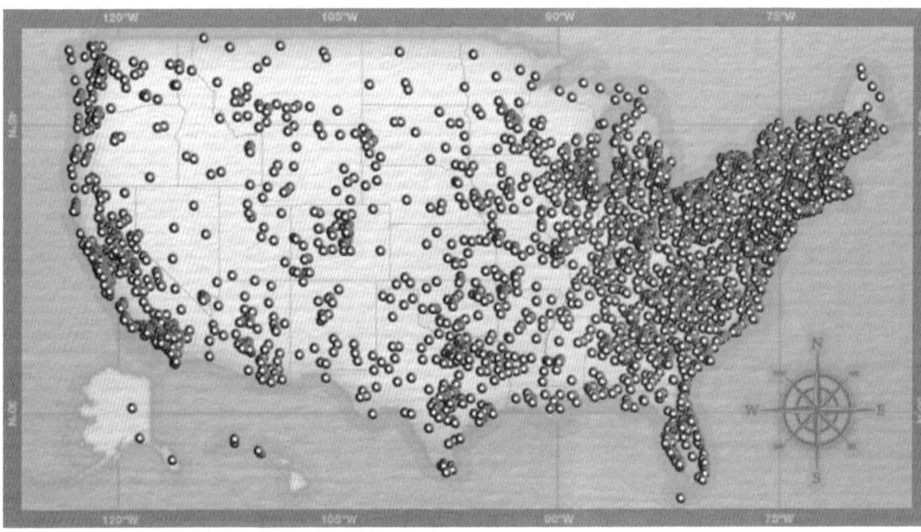

Search for your hometown history, your old stomping grounds, and even your favorite sports team.

Consistent with our mission to preserve history on a local level, this book was printed in South Carolina on American-made paper and manufactured entirely in the United States. Products carrying the accredited Forest Stewardship Council (FSC) label are printed on 100 percent FSC-certified paper.

MADE IN THE USA